• ACCLAIM FOR *businessThink* •

businessThink skillfully outlines fundamental business principals for the successful business organization. It offers practical concepts and progressive thinking. Read it for your success! (Unless you are comfortable with business as usual—looking forward to playing politics, flexing your ego, and pounding your way up the corporate ladder. . . .)

> **—Horst H. Schulze**
> Former Vice Chairman, Ritz-Carlton Hotel Company, LLC

What makes this book so useful is that it offers a heavy dose of something important but in short supply in business today—common sense.

> **—Jack Trout**
> Author, *Differentiate or Die*

Survey people on their driving skills. No one admits to less than good practices, yet crashes—both business and vehicle—prove otherwise. *businessThink* is a deceptively simple yet insightful reference book, which, if honestly applied, has the potential to impact that critical space between thinking and action or [inaction]. For those who apply the learning from *businessThink,* there is as much to be gained in the public sector as in the corporate community.

> **—Patricia Pelton**
> CEO, Northern Lights Regional Health Authority
> Fort McMurray, Alberta

This book is needed today more than ever before, in this business climate where every employee in every organization must businessThink, business-Act, and businessWork like they are the CEO!

> **—Gregory Coleman**
> Executive Vice President of North American Operations,
> Yahoo!

Occasionally there comes a book that doesn't "descend" from on high in academia, but arises from the blood, sweat, and tears of the trenches of reality and makes such powerful sense that it opens our eyes to how our businesses really should be run. *businessThink* is that book.

> **—Dr. Charles Roadman**
> CEO, American Health Care Association
> Former Surgeon General, U.S. Air Force

businessThink focuses on where success starts: with the thinking process. In simple straightforward language, authors Dave Marcum, Steve Smith, and Mahan Khalsa present a process to transform the way people think about business. A must read for everyone.

> **—Stedman Graham**
> Author, *You Can Make It Happen*
> Chairman and CEO, S. Graham & Associates

Lucidly presented, the authors' rules of engagement will unearth the hidden psychology that keeps companies from succeeding despite—or maybe because of—their best ideas.

> **—Larry Downes**
> Coauthor, *Unleashing the Killer App*

businessThink is a gem. Its "common sense" is in fact very uncommon sense. Follow the eight rules the authors derived from their research and consulting, and you'll dramatically up the odds of success—and the joy that flows from work well done.

> **—Tom Peters**
> Author, *In Search of Excellence*

businessThink is insightful, wise, and easy to grasp. I recommend this book to anyone interested in exploring effective problem-solving solutions.

> **—Rich DeVos**
> Cofounder, Amway Corporation
> Owner and Chairman, NBA Orlando Magic

Intelligence and attitude are the only things you need to get ahead in the business world. You can't do much about your intelligence, but you can read *businessThink,* which will do wonders for your attitude.

> **—Al Ries**
> Coauthor, *Positioning*

businessThink is a practical, pragmatic guide to better business decisions. Managers should read the book with their teams and use it in leading team implementation of the wisdom it contains.

> **—Bill Hitchcock**
> Global Director, EDS Digital Learning Services
> SmartExecutive E-Learning Executive of the Year, 2001

businessThink . . . could very well, in my opinion, qualify as the 8th Habit of Highly Effective People. The book is simply brilliant . . . a true leader's roadmap in leveraging and maximizing the intellectual capitalism of today's business person.

> **—Pete Beaudrault**
> President and CEO, Hard Rock Café International

businessThink is every person's MBA for the real world. It takes straight aim at the decades of dysfunction in business and hits the mark with a real-world "degree" of pragmatic, new thinking for new times.

> **—Tom Curley**
> CEO and Publisher, *USA Today*

Thinking is hard. Thinking creatively is harder. Thinking creatively about business is hardest. This book not only enlightens you from hard to hardest, but does it with profound simplicity.

> **—Warren Bennis,**
> Author, *Managing the Dream*
> Distinguished Professor of Business Administration,
> University of Southern California

This is a great book and an easy read. It enhances the productivity of everyone who follows the advice given in it. It will release the energy of people in organizations. It is a must for every leader to have everyone in his organization practice the principals in this book.

> **—Dr. Ram Charan**
> Author, *What the CEO Wants You to Know*

The lessons of *businessThink* are understandable and actionable. If your organization—like ours—wants to be recognized as the best, this book should be required reading for all current and future business leaders and managers.

> **—William G. Parrett**
> President and Managing Partner, Deloitte & Touche LLP

In today's competitive business environments, *businessThink* should be required reading for employees at all levels. . . . It describes how to take responsibility for where you're going and how to get there, relevant for all facets of your life. . . . *businessThink* goes places other business books are afraid to go.

> **—Dave Gregory**
> President and CEO, First Calgary Savings

In a world that demands single-minded focus and disciplined, fact-based decisions at warp speed, *businessThink* provides a common-sense, jargon-free return to the core concept of creating real value in business.

> **—Gary Crittenden**
> Chief Financial Officer, American Express Company

businessThink

businessThink

Rules for Getting It Right—
Now, and No Matter What!

Dave Marcum
Steve Smith
Mahan Khalsa

Foreword by Stephen R. Covey

John Wiley & Sons, Inc.

Published by John Wiley & Sons, Inc., New York.
Published simultaneously in Canada.

This publication is designed to provide accurate and authoritative information in regard to the subject matter covered. It is sold with the understanding that the publisher is not engaged in rendering professional services. If professional advice or other expert assistance is required, the services of a competent professional person should be sought.

Library of Congress Cataloging-in-Publication Data:
Marcum, Dave.
    businessThink : rules for getting it right—now, and no matter what! / by Dave Marcum, Steve Smith and Mahan Khalsa.
      p.   cm.
    "Published simultaneously in Canada."
    ISBN 0-471-21993-2 (cloth : alk. paper)
    1. Success in business.   2. Decision making.   I. Title: Rules for getting it right—now, and no matter what!.   II. Smith, Steve.   III. Khalsa, Mahan.   IV. Title.
HF5386 .S694 2002
650.1—dc21   2001008001

Printed in the United States of America.

10 9 8 7 6 5 4 3 2 1

• THE AGENDA •

• FOREWORD •

In the Middle Ages, the Western world viewed bloodletting as one of the best means of healing the sick. Because physicians believed that illnesses existed in "bad blood," they systematically bled people to rid them of illness. If the patient's condition didn't improve, the logic of bloodletting simply dictated that they should do more—they just had to do it better this time. This way of thinking persisted even into the early twentieth century.

Now, what if we were to apply today's hottest, most powerful management ideas to the challenge of making bloodletting practices more effective? What if we applied quality control and statistical analysis to bloodletting techniques? Or how about organizing team-building workshops for bloodletting physicians and technicians? You could take the trained medical people of the Bloodletting Unit to the hills, let them do free falls into each others' arms and work on building trust. You could implement an empowerment program so that the members of the unit would have greater latitude in developing innovative tools and methodologies for bloodletting. Better yet, you could conduct positive mental attitude (PMA) training for both patients and medical personnel in order to build stronger symbiotic patient–physician relationships, and then both parties could exude greater positive energy during the procedures. The result? It's laughable. Sure, the Bloodletting Unit would optimize bloodletting efficiency, and everyone would be happy and efficient—that is, everyone but the dead patients and their loved ones!

Thankfully, empirical science led to the *germ theory*. Ignaz Semmelweis of Hungary and Louis Pasteur of France brilliantly developed this simple, commonsense explanation of the cause and means of prevention of infection. For the first time, physicians understood why women preferred to have their babies delivered by midwives—the midwives washed their hands! Physicians finally understood why more men died from disease behind the front lines than from bullets on the battlefield. A new, revolutionary paradigm shifted their thinking. The age of bloodletting was forever gone, and a new, life-saving paradigm of science replaced the old paradigm.

This part of human history illustrates a very simple principle: The key to powerful breakthroughs is not simply to change your behavior—it's not enough to change your attitude; it's necessary to change how you *see* the world, your paradigm, the assumptions you make. All the great transformations in history have come primarily from paradigm shifts—from changing the way people see things. I've learned over the years that if you want to make small, incremental changes, work on *behavior* or *attitude*. However, if you want to make quantum changes or improvements, work on *paradigms*.

Significant progress and breakthrough results come as we examine our paradigms, our thinking, and remain open to changes from the inside out. But this is risky business! Many private victories that deepen our inner security, courage, and humility must first be won before we can afford the emotional risk-taking that produces the great public victories. Anwar Sadat once said, "He who cannot change the very fabric of his thought will never be able to change reality, and will never, therefore, make any progress."

What are *our* paradigms today in the business world? Are we making significant progress? If not, what is holding us back? Are we achieving breakthrough performance and results? What are *our* modern-day management equivalents of bloodletting?

It is absolutely vital to have a process for regularly examining your paradigms to survive and thrive in today's turbulent world. Each day brings a new challenge demanding a response that is equal to it. When the response is equal to the challenge, you have success. The problem is that when a new, greater challenge arises, the tendency is to use the patterns, processes, and practices that have brought success in the past. However, often these patterns, processes, and practices no longer work. To quote Arnold Toynbee, one of the greatest historians of our time, "Nothing fails like success."

Consider today's challenges. The world is changing at unthinkable speed. Uncertainty rules the day. Many new ideas and products face the likelihood of being obsolete at, or shortly following, their launch. Industries have been revolutionized by technology. Entire business sectors have been wiped out or have thoroughly transformed themselves in order to remain relevant. A global marketplace with global competition puts many industries and organizations at the mercy of fluctuating global economies. Customers are fickle and brand loyalty is hard to sustain. Companies have to manage in the face of crisis, and employees demand greater opportunities for self-leadership. Perhaps most dramatic of all, whereas information was once autocratic and guarded by an elite few, information today is universally democratized—and there is an unstoppable demand for participative and democratic systems in all sectors of society.

What can we rely on in this new world? I suggest there are only three reliable constants in life: (1) *change,* (2) *principles,* and (3) *choice*—the power that we have to adapt and respond to the first two constants. The greatest need we have in a world that changes at the "speed of thought" is for something that does not change: principles. Unchanging principles, like a compass that points to true north, enable us to navigate in the face of change and the new dynamics of a global marketplace.

Relentless change is certainly a fact of life. However, how we choose to respond to change is an entirely different proposition. As we examine the business world today, what pragmatic choices must we make to be successful? Can we get breakthrough results without some *break-withs*—breaks with old ways of thinking? The challenging realities of our changing world demand principle-centered solutions that are equal to our present and future challenges.

I believe that *businessThink* presents a provocative, principle-centered paradigm shift for radically rethinking the way we do business. For some time now, the business world has made incremental progress in finding better leadership and management practices, but for too long we seem to have remained on a plateau. Why? Why is it that innovation, as the authors so convincingly suggest, is at history's highest level, but business failures are, too? Why is there such a gap between generating terrific ideas and actually executing them successfully?

Part of the answer can be found in the abstract nature of our solutions to new problems. Too many of us (myself included) become entrenched in abstract models that do not always make the leap to the tangible. It may be this disconnect between the *why* and the *how* that has created this gap. But with *businessThink*, the gap is bridged, because it provides not only the abstract or conceptual but also the schematic and empirical framework. In short, the paradigm shift is from the hypothetical to real-life application.

Steve Smith, Dave Marcum, and Mahan Khalsa masterfully create a compelling case for changing the way we look at problems and opportunities, for changing the way we make decisions, and for changing the things we do. *businessThink* introduces a powerful, yet simple, framework for achieving breakthrough results. First, *businessThink* breaks the old "business-as-usual" rules, which we've too often blindly followed or lazily accepted. Then, through a sequential process of *disciplined* thinking, this new framework teaches us how to gain clarity of mind and heart, and how to get it right—no excuses. In fact, I'm convinced that using the principles of *businessThink* can significantly increase your effectiveness and success in *any* area of your life. I have personally experienced an exciting paradigm shift, and I am greatly encouraged by the prospects of *businessThink*.

Unleashing Human Potential

In his book, *Management Challenges of the 21st Century,* management scholar Peter Drucker observes:

> The most important, and indeed the truly unique, contribution of management in the 20th century was the fifty-fold increase in the productivity of the MANUAL WORKER in manufacturing.
>
> The most important contribution management needs to make in the 21st century is similarly to increase the productivity *of the* KNOWLEDGE WORKER.

Such quantum leaps in productivity will come only when we tap into the mind, body, heart, and spirit of people, and when leadership is seen as an enabling art—an art that communicates to people their worth and potential so clearly that they are inspired to see it in themselves. The bottom line is that human capital (intellectual *and* social) is the most valuable asset of any organization. The challenge is to unleash the minds and hearts of people toward greater creativity, productivity, and results. And it is, in fact, the paradigm and leadership style of the supervisor or manager that defines the manual worker or knowledge worker. Choose to see all employees as knowledge workers—then teach them to businessThink—and you will find yourself surrounded by energized knowledge workers.

For instance, take a janitor's job—a so-called low-level, unimportant job. Surely, businessThink or other models don't apply to such positions. But wait: Don't the janitors have the same four parts of human nature—body, mind, heart, and spirit—as any other employees? Why not treat all workers with the same paradigm? Involve the janitors in the planning; in fact, turn the planning over to them. Let the janitors select the materials; let them organize a work schedule and create the criteria for completing and evaluating tasks. In essence, let the janitors run their business! You will find that when people are given the directed autonomy to set the criteria, methods, and evaluation process, they are usually tougher on themselves than others would be. Let them manage their work and let them evaluate their own performance against the criteria you've developed together, and you will find greater results.

Now you've got janitors with true, internal motivation, using all four parts of their nature. They are whole persons in a whole job. They are knowledge workers. In reality, they always have been knowledge workers, but others are just now realizing it. (I share this example not as a hypothetical one but as a true story. And it clearly illustrates the power of the whole-person paradigm working in any job or circumstance.)

There is no doubt that the knowledge worker deserves to be treated as a whole person—a self-directed human being who has intellectual *and* emotional intelligence with potential for growth— someone who has the power and freedom to choose and who aspires to achieve a valuable purpose. Indeed, the knowledge worker has great capabilities and great expectations. When leaders and managers believe in and reinforce these capabilities and expectations, you will most often find tremendous individual, human potential being released. Only then do you see *enduring* breakthrough performance and results produced.

Every Person's MBA

businessThinking is a powerful method for unleashing this human potential. Regardless of position, status, rank, or file, *anyone* can use this model and its eight accompanying rules to get remarkable results. For too long, we have depended on a few "top" minds to solve our pressing business problems (and not always successfully). The rest of us go through the motions of *doing*, but perhaps not really *thinking*, and therefore, not fully *achieving*. With business-Think, *every* employee in an organization may develop the business acumen to think, investigate, discover, and act. Never before have I seen a framework that so disciplines our mind-set and heart to balance logic and pragmatism with intuition and idealism. In a sense, it is every person's MBA—an MBA for the real world.

These authors teach business for the real world—they are entrepreneurs who have owned their own businesses; they have been employees of small to large companies; and they have been consultants for various industries. They have been in the throes of running successful and failed organizations. They have been around the block. They have succeeded and they have failed—and they're refreshingly honest and open about their successes and, perhaps most importantly, their failures. These authors perhaps represent the new mind-set of the Internet generation, which is highly technical and rigorous, but also intuitive enough to grasp the roots of effective human relations. Clearly, they have developed conscious competence by striking on principles of effectiveness—by way of research *and* by sheer experience—and their work is an innovative, fresh, and lively look into the realities of the business world.

In addition to bringing greater clarity to business, *businessThink* also reminds us that business should be fun. If not entirely fun, it ought to be, at its core, a creative adventure. It is easy and exciting to discern the adventurous nature of the authors as they explore the business world and share their insights. They have an unusual knack for creating excitement around a rigorous discipline that reminds people to *think clearly and deeply.*

No Margin, No Mission

I once attended a board meeting conducted by a CEO facing painful challenges. Layer by layer, this CEO built his case for rethinking the organization's core strategy. He asked questions that allowed him to say less and listen more. Then he asked more questions, digging deeper and deeper for answers. His mind was honed and disciplined with facts, data, and evidence, but he also kindly addressed the questions, fears, and discomfort of the change process. Because he carefully took the group through each level of thinking, placing the issues at hand in context, all present were led to understand the pressing economic reality: *no margin, no mission.*

Through this painstaking process, the CEO was able to present his case as though he were before a jury—providing the hard evidence but doing so with a keen sense of respect and dignity for the best judgment of the jury. Clearly, he was a leader who blended the best in EQ (emotional quotient) and IQ (intelligence quotient), and he eventually won the support and commitment of the board.

As I looked back at this board meeting, I came away with a clearer sense of what it means to be effective—to blend disciplined, investigative thinking with a heartfelt, intuitive ability to build high-trust relationships. This level of effectiveness is accomplished by balancing EQ (kind-heartedness) with IQ (tough-mindedness). I would bet that the leaders or people who have most influenced you and your life are those who possess this EQ/IQ acumen.

This acumen has taken a name today—it is called businessThink.

Of course, it isn't enough for one person, the CEO, to possess businessThink qualities. True, lasting change and long-term success come only from *institutionalizing* best practices and principles into the systems, structures, processes and culture of an organization. businessThink acumen can be cultivated throughout an organization's *culture* by planting in the minds and hearts of employees a belief that things can be done in a new way—teaching them to think outside their own situations, outside their jobs, so they can see the larger picture of the business itself. Simply, *businessThink* teaches everyone in an organization to be a knowledge worker—someone who fully understands the business; someone who is encouraged to think and feel deeply; someone who is unleashed towards creativity, innovation, and results.

businessThink not only illuminates the need for a new business model, it goes a vital step further by teaching the reader *how* to do it. It is in this instruction that businessThink can be institutionalized in *any* organization—and herein lies its remarkable power.

Disciplined Decision Making

Every endeavor begins with an idea. Good business is propelled by good ideas that are translated into good decisions. The best decisions are made when people look beyond their own cubicles, considering their entire organization and the possible business impact.

This requires business savvy and seeing success as an *ecological* phenomenon—a framework that considers the needs of *all* stakeholders as integral parts of a larger, whole entity. businessThink presents a definitive and sequential process for understanding that you have to have success in the workplace *and* in the marketplace jointly in order to have success in the capital marketplace and with the shareholders. The ultimate mantra of the public CEO is *shareholder value*. But producing shareholder value requires this ecological balance between knowledge workers, the workplace, the culture, the marketplace, and the customers. These are absolutely indivisible parts, and focusing only on one part causes a critical imbalance, which will ultimately hurt the outcome.

Language of the Effective CEO

I will conclude by repeating that businessThink is the language of effective CEOs worldwide. Find any highly successful and effective CEO, and you will naturally find the principles of businessThink at work. Dig deeper, and you will find that *any* effective leader—whether in government, the community, the school, the family, or in business—is a businessThinker. These leaders are people who balance disciplined thinking with intuition. They ask questions, explore for answers, dig for deeper meaning and context, and at the same time they genuinely build integrity, trust, compassion, synergy, and respect in their relationships. businessThinkers are also mindful to teach these commonsense principles to others, thereby building greater, more powerful thinking capacity in the organization. Clearly, these people work in a third alternative way—simultaneously kind-hearted, and tough-minded—emulating the best in businessThinking.

The authors are quick to acknowledge that businessThink is a compilation of learning from many individuals, organizations, institutions, books, leaders, writers, coworkers, family, friends, and people in general. Its theory is developed primarily from the trenches. What is refreshing to me is that by being disciplined and faithful students, the authors are also great teachers. And great teachers are ultimately good examples or models of what they teach. So, again, this all boils down to the fact that you can learn to businessThink your way to effectiveness and success in any area of your life and in any undertaking. Furthermore, you can model these principles and teach others to be businessThinkers—creating exponential power for evolving pragmatic, new thinking for new times.

Stephen R. Covey

• ACKNOWLEDGMENTS •

The last words written that go into a book are the acknowledgments, and they are placed up front—and rightly so. Winston Churchill once said that writing a book goes through five phases. In the first phase it is a novelty or a toy, and by phase five it becomes a tyrant that rules your life. The people we want to thank have given efforts that added so much, made our own efforts better, and helped us tame the tyrant, and so they deserve the spotlight first. In bringing out the spotlight, sometimes there are things in life you are so deeply grateful for that there are no words to communicate your feelings. There is no thesaurus big enough to help us express our thanks adequately, so our words will barely do justice to what we hope to say. We'll still give it our best shot.

Lynn Frost   Few people are able to rise to the level of brilliance in their craft. Lynn's directorial brilliance was much needed, deeply appreciated, and a major force in shaping businessThink early on. Spending much of his personal time in reading early manuscripts, Lynn also helped us find what we thought would be the easiest thing to come by—our voice. When our writing and style wasn't congruent with the content we were writing about or who we are as people, he called us on it. Whenever we drifted from real-life practice into authorspeak, he screamed for practicality. He always seemed able to identify the key points we needed to communicate but were obscured and needed to be set free.

Bryce Thacker   In any company, there is noise and interference that must be recognized and plowed through, or it gets in the way of people creating value. Bryce willingly entered war zones to fight battles in our behalf, lived through it, and, most important, had the wisdom to not tell us about many of the battles that were being waged. He ably kept us far behind the firing lines and allowed us to focus on our writing. He helped us shape the business plans and financial analysis that were required to get support inside our company. He also offered timely words of encouragement and enthusiasm when we needed it most and when it felt as if no one else was on our side.

Greg Link   Few words can describe the relief and confidence we were afforded by having a partner like Greg. As a master of the book industry, his savvy was a blessing to us from the beginning. He has been immensely helpful (mammoth understatement) in helping us understand the nuances of book publishing and marketing, and contract and book negotiations. He helped us to know what we needed and, perhaps more important, what we didn't need. Greg was a much-needed confidant. He was positive and capable, and has been a life-saving partner in reminding us of the importance of staying sequestered to do what we do best in the final stages of writing.

Airié Dekidjiev   When we were shopping our manuscript and met with the people at John Wiley, we thought we had a book. Using publishing lingo, Airié called it a *proposal*. She has helped us transform our proposal into a book, and has become a significant force in pushing us to make our ideas clear and to do more than we thought possible. Her exceptional editorial organizational ability has made the important ideas in the content easier to access and recognize. From the very first day we met, she was enthusiastic about our work. She carried that enthusiasm to others in her organization. Thankfully, she has been patient as we have exhibited our author's enthusiasm and intense passion.

Stephen M. R. Covey   It's often not easy to see the potential in people or work, especially in the early stages. It may be especially difficult when your father is the best-selling business author of all time. Stephen has been a great supporter and has walked with and encouraged us in our "last mile" to create value for our company and the business world. Not only has he been a passionate advocate for businessThink, he is a capable dealmaker. Stephen has an enviable ability to think beyond the usual limitations most people have when it comes to bringing two sides together. Were it not for him, this book would be brought to you by someone other than FranklinCovey.

Jan Miller As our book agent, Jan took a risk on us as unknown authors. Her experience and insight made the process of finding a publisher efficient, effective, and fun. She put us in front of the top publishing companies in the world and helped us pick the one best suited to our needs. She was an advocate for businessThink early on, and we are grateful for her early vision.

Thanks also to **Annie Oswald** for her hard work and assistance on this project.

Everyone else The list is huge here. Dozens of people read the manuscript, racing against impossible deadlines, and gave us feedback that helped us refine our thinking and break out of the "good" to hit the great. Initially, we liked the nice feedback and ultimately found the greatest value in the candid feedback that was both positive and negative. Many of these unnamed contributors will recognize their input or suggestions in the text, and some of their influence won't be so obvious to them. Nonetheless, every comment was carefully considered, and this book is much better because of their unique perspectives. We could name names, and we would miss people. Besides, we intend to thank each one personally, because saying "Thanks everyone!" and leaving it at only that is kind of, well, lame.

Steve's Personal Thanks

> *Those who dream by night wake to find it was vanity. But the dreamers of the day are dangerous men, for they may act out their dream with open eyes to make it possible.*
> —T. E. Lawrence (Lawrence of Arabia), *Seven Pillars of Wisdom*

I'm glad I daydreamed, and would like to thank a few people for help making it possible. First, I would personally like to dedicate this book to my supportive, talented, beautiful wife, Kitty. I love you and could not have done this without you—literally! I would also like to deeply thank my three "pups" at home: Coker, Cady Bug, and my li'l pup, Nicky Kicker. They have gone weeks without seeing Dad, and have sacrificed time with me they won't get back. Being reminded on September 11, 2001, how short life can be, it makes it all the more of a sacrifice on their part. In addition, I would like to thank Tom Peters for inspiring me to do this, Kim Peterson for pushing me to raise my own XQ years ago, and U2 for writing great music and sparking my brain when I thought hitting the wall would be my last hit. I guess every writer breaks out of a rut and gets back in the groove some way. I usually found it at high decibels with great music and lyrics. In some ways, not having a great voice or a poetic mind, my lyrics and music have become businessThink.

Last, but not least, I would also like to thank everyone who does truly great work, no matter where you are. I've been inspired by great authors, exceptional movies, creative ads, brilliant commercials, insightful biographies, inspired art, unbelievable music, and extraordinary athletes. Genius, no matter where it is found or in what arena, is inspiring. Everybody is brilliant at something, and there is something very pristine and rejuvenating when you see and feel it. The transformative power of their craft exceeds its "functional" boundaries and has shaped and molded me. Last, but certainly not least, to everyone who cares about their work and craves to make it better. Bravo! "This is the real world, muchachos, and we should all *change* it. . . ."

Dave's Personal Thanks

I would like to dedicate this book to my family, which is my greatest treasure. To my beautiful wife Karen, you easily draw from me and deserve my undying love and appreciation. In my absence, you have carried the heavy load, emotional and otherwise, by yourself and have spent many lonely nights without me so I could teach workshops, write, learn, and grow. Thank you for your unquestioned support and love. To my children, Lindsay, Jeffrey and Spencer, thank you, too, for your support and encouragement. You each gave up being able to spend time with me, which I love, and you missed out on having me there for some of your important moments in life. You are such an important part of my life and I missed you. I also want to thank my mom and dad. The older I get the more I realize how much they sacrificed for me and I took it for granted or was ungrateful. Please know how deeply I love you. Thank you for giving me and teaching me so much.

Last, thanks to many leaders and colleagues who have endured me, dug trenches with me, coached me, taught me, and inspired me. I hope you find this book personally valuable and helpful. In the spirit of wanting to give back to you, this book is a symbolic effort to repay what you have given me.

businessThink

The Innovation Explosion

The world is more innovative than ever. Technology that once required mammoth-size hardware now fits in the palm of your hand. Diseases thought to be incurable are now on their way to being wiped out thanks to revolutionary biotech research. Imagination, ideas, and discoveries continue to flood the planet in remarkable ways and at unbelievable speed.

With great hope and expectations, inventors and entrepreneurs all over the world breathe life into ingenious ideas and pioneer new businesses every day. Companies are driven by the minute to break new ground with products and services that will give them a competitive edge.

> Globally, every 60 minutes 101 new patents are applied for, and over 2,265 new businesses are started every day.[1]

Although we've grown accustomed to it, we are witnessing one of the greatest innovation explosions in history. The climate for new ideas and inventions continues to create big-time excitement and optimism in business. Eighty-one percent of entrepreneurs are optimistic about the prospects of success for their companies.[2] Despite the roller-coaster ride of an unpredictable economy, there is a strong sense of confidence in the business world—the optimism that no doubt comes from faith and trust in the power of innovation.

The Business Implosion

Note the contrast between that confidence in the midst of the innovation explosion and the diametrically opposed results—the business implosion. As quickly as ideas pop up, and as rapidly as new companies open for business, failure takes them down.

> By the time you finish reading this introduction, over 46 businesses will have ceased operating, and 3 will have filed for bankruptcy. By the end of the day, over 2,131 new businesses will have followed their lead.[3]

By the minute, companies admit poor financial performance, followed by layoffs and countless versions of restructuring efforts—face-lift after face-lift until the companies, themselves, are unrecognizable.

Equal to the number of good ideas being unleashed is the number of bad ideas—many of which are quietly and quickly killed. Ever heard of Cracker Jack cereal, Ben-Gay aspirin, or Smucker's ketchup?[4] Our point exactly. There is a proliferation of inductees into the unsuccessful product (or idea) hall of fame, and they just keep coming. Even innovative ideas don't guarantee an "Open for Business" sign on the front door.

Here's a sobering thought: In spite of intense innovation, success rates aren't getting any better—research continues to show that every time we start one new venture, nearly four fail.[5] Currently, there is a monumental gap between generating ideas and getting results.

So why do so many good ideas fail? Why do so many bad ideas make it to production? Why is it that innovation doesn't guarantee success, and why do bright, determined entrepreneurs fall way short? Ideas continue to heat up while business continues to melt down. What gives?

Thinking: The Big Bang of Business

What's caving in on business today is our thinking (or lack of it). The most amazing and powerful asset in business—the human mind—hasn't been equipped or taught to think *business*. The results you get in business come directly from the choices you make about what activities get your time and attention. At some point, given unlimited choices and limited time, you decide to do some things and let others go; your effectiveness is often driven as much by the things you don't do and should as by the things that you actually do and shouldn't. Ultimately, your decisions are driven by your thinking.

> *Thinking is the nucleus of business—it drives not only what gets created and launched, but also what lives on. It's the "big bang" that sets everything else in motion. If you want to change your results, you must first change your thinking.*

However, most people are just going through the motions of *doing* (not thinking) business—merely practicing their comfortable, old routines of business, or "doing their jobs," while others, the really successful ones, are actually getting killer results through changing their thinking to become more disciplined, rigorous, creative, and sound.

Our Lessons from the Street

We've been where many of you are now, in the trenches of business. We've worked as rank-and-file employees, started our own companies, experienced failure and success, battled egos (often our own), and plowed through politics. As consultants we have been in and out of companies, large and small, around the world over the last two decades. We've been a part of phenomenal meetings where everyone was "on," crafting brilliant strategy, thinking clearly, communicating openly, and innovating ideas that lifted the enterprise to a new level. We've also watched our own companies, and our clients, miss big opportunities and live with chronic business problems that have gone unsolved. These are organizations that may never wake up to what caused the gap between what they wanted and what they got. We've seen confusion *and* brilliance working with companies like Nike, Microsoft, Hard Rock Cafe, EDS, William M. Mercer, the United Nations, and city and state governments across the country. It is the contrast between the good and the truly great businesspeople that made us all the more passionate about what emerged as businessThink.

In our pursuit to build businessThink, we didn't study organizations. We studied *people:* the interactions within strategy meetings, team projects, and conversations. We watched what worked and what got in the way, and what developed was a set of rules that separated the average businesspeople from the truly brilliant ones.

The rules can be the acid test for every product researched and developed, idea funded, alliance formed, merger contemplated, operational overhaul implemented, management theory espoused, and strategy adopted.

As consultants with FranklinCovey, we've applied the rules of businessThink in a wide variety of roles and settings; everything from sales and consulting, to marketing, to project implementation, to running a business unit. We've taught these rules in over 40 countries around the world, and found that they hold true no matter where you are or what kind of organization you're in.

For example, one of our clients, the United Nations, was interested in equipping its offices in developing countries with the businessThinking skills needed to handle the increasingly complex and sophisticated development going on in the third world. Even in the world of not-for-profit organizations, what used to be a no-brainer—you would stick out your hand for money and donors (nations, companies, individuals) would write big checks—isn't the norm anymore. Blank checks are not so much standard operating procedure as was once the case in the charity and not-for-profit world. Now not-for-profits and similar organizations, like the United Nations, must compete with other large, well-organized organizations such as the World Bank, regional banks, and non-governmental organizations to get their share of resources to fund operations to deal with issues such as HIV/AIDS, human rights, environmental degradation, and the like. In this global economy and environment, all organizations—and especially not-for-profit organizations—need to reprofile themselves to be relevant to the issues in each country or specialty area. Many charities and government organizations must become more businessThinking in order to better develop and present business cases for their solutions.

In government, tax cuts, programs, policies, procedures, and laws are only as good as the fundamental, underlying issues they address. Imagine how effective government would be if politicians and bureaucrats alike moved off their agendas and proposed solutions, got evidence to prove their cases, calculated the impact on their constituencies, considered the obstacles before implementing solutions, and found the real, underlying causes of problems or opportunities for implementing their ideas. Everyone must become a businessperson, even if they're not in traditionally business-minded organizations.

> **Among businesspeople with different languages and cultures, and among diverse organizations, the rules produce the same results: increased leverage of time, better allocation of resources, strategic decisions, mapping products and services to targeted business results, increased business acumen, solutions to critical problems, and choosing the right priorities.**

Imagine how challenging it is to start a business—and the numbers aren't exactly in your favor in the first place. Now imagine starting a new business when the stock market index has just tumbled 30 percent, currency has been devalued to 60 percent, and the budget of most companies for your product has been cut by 80 percent. Not exactly the most favorable conditions (and probably overwhelming to most), yet those were the conditions in South Korea in 1998. Prominent businesspeople who were used to suits and Mercedes-Benzes traded them in for waiter's aprons and bus passes.

A colleague of ours in South Korea is a prime example of a great businessThinker. He entered those market conditions with nothing more than determination and a commitment to fundamentally change the way he and his colleagues were thinking in their own business. He viewed the challenge in the tradition of an ancient Chinese proverb: During any *crisis* (危机) two possibilities exist— the *danger* (危險) of bankruptcy, or the *opportunity* (机會) for a quantum leap. He and his colleagues had been teaching those very principles to their clients, and the time had arrived to walk the talk. In sales and marketing, they moved off the solutions they had been doing business by and considered what underlying issues they should address in a new and changing economy. Doing so allowed them to look at things they hadn't considered in a strong economy: focusing sales only on high-probability clients who needed new approaches and thinking, firms that were profiting at a higher exchange rate, and international firms that were more stable globally.

They also made keen observations and collected evidence in their own market that demonstrated why the economy was suffering, what their clients could do about it, and what impact the changes could have on their clients' companies. Internally, our colleague asked everyone to cross their own functional boundaries: Everyone was in sales, everyone was in advertising—everyone was a living, breathing, and businessThinking entrepreneur. Everyone worked hard to find leveraged activities and then focused on them. They were determined to show and prove that the crisis really *was* an opportunity. Since businessThinking, they have enjoyed a 50 to 70 percent growth rate for the first three years and are expecting the same for the future. Their success, given the economic gloom they faced, gave new meaning to the phrase, "These were the best of times, they were the worst of times."

If you live the rules, the same kind of success will be yours.

Eight Rules, New Instincts

Here, in short, are the rules you're about to dive into understanding and beginning to practice (see Fig. I.1):

1. Check Your Ego at the Door.
2. Create Curiosity.
3. Move Off the Solution.
4. Get Evidence.
5. Calculate the Impact.
6. Explore the Ripple Effect.
7. Slow Down for Yellow Lights.
8. Find the Cause.

Our hope is that these eight rules will be the seeds of a much-needed revolution in business and will cultivate a fundamentally new way of thinking, communicating, and deciding in business, no matter where you are in the world, and no matter at what level you are at in your organization. You are constantly bombarded by the

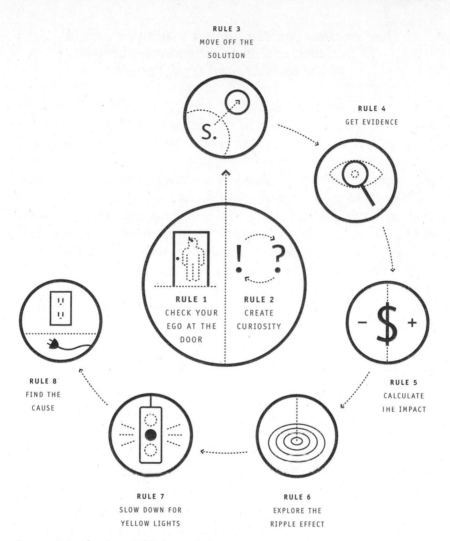

Figure I.1   businessThink model.

pressure to get it right—now, and no matter what. It's up to you to make the right decisions, fund the right projects, land on the right strategy, or hire the right person. You've been expected to get it right even though you've lacked all the tools you need. businessThink will give you the business tools to transform *what* you think about, and how you ultimately decide what you *should* be doing, and eliminate the distraction of what you *could* be doing.

> *Just because you can doesn't mean you should!*
> *In business,* coulds *are the sworn enemies*
> *of the* shoulds, *and trash results.*

Every day, you are not only expected to think your way to results—part of your task is to increasingly build the capacity of other people inside your organization. With businessThink, you can help anyone to think sharply, fluently, and comprehensively about getting answers on their own, without losing sight of both the bigger picture and their own contributing role. For a long time a select few ran organizations, and everyone else simply followed orders. There are leftover habits from earlier business times—such as a near-fanatical devotion to hierarchy—that corrupt thinking.

The old rules breed dependency, not interdependence and collaboration, and run thinking and decisions into the ground. businessThink will help you even if, and especially if, those around you and above you don't live by the rules.

businessThink versus Business School

Years ago we went to business school to learn the rules of business. We enjoyed it. We learned a lot, and graduated with the optimism that most graduates leave with. We now realize that our secondary education was a bit *too* secondary to what really happens once you hit the corporate scene.

> School gives you a technical ticket into the stadium and helps you understand the written rules and language of business, but it can't possibly fully prepare you for the unwritten rules of *doing* business.

The changes needed for *doing* business effectively have been blocked by the dysfunction of the real business world. On an individual level, fear, ego, facades, lazy thinking, and generally bad habits of communication keep everyone from getting it right as much as they want and desperately need. Dramatically changing the way we all do business for the better will require moving beyond mild modification to nothing less than the complete abandonment of old, ineffective conventions. As Dee Hock, a great business visionary and the creator of Visa, once said:

> *The problem is never how to get new,*
> *innovative thoughts into your mind,*
> *but how to get the old ones out.*[6]

As you take on the new thought processes proposed in *businessThink,* you'll also need to get old ones out of your head. We won't teach you the "right" answers, but the way you can get the right answers. One of the designs of businessThink is to bring flexibility to some things in business that are too rigid, and to bring order to a process that is often chaotic. businessThink is our answer to the big question of how to be "on" all the time at work. This is the real-life business class we wish we'd had, but never got.

This is a making-it-happen—now, and no matter what—book. Because, as the old saying goes, "easier said than done" (that's why so much is said!), we will offer specifics on everything from how to illustrate a point to how to ask a specific question, and even walk through possible dialogue for a host of business scenarios. Part of thinking effectively in (and about) business requires an expanded business vocabulary. The new language comes from years of practice and application, and we'll share specific examples of dialogue because the language often has to be precise in order to be effective.

If you like what you see in results, and businessThink makes sense to you, live it *out loud* and make it your own. John F. Kennedy said, "Each time you stand up for [a principle] you send forth a ripple of hope." The seeds of revolution are often best sown by common people doing uncommon, extraordinary things—and not just once or twice, but time after time. If you do *live* these rules (and our invitation is to live them passionately), they will become instinctual.

> **You will develop a business instinct or seventh sense for knowing what works and what doesn't long before you spend the time, people, and money to really find out.**

As you live by these rules, the people around you will adapt to your soon-to-be natural instincts. Your results and the environment you work in will change.

Not Dilbert's World

Imagine what the future could be like. Suppose you walked into your first meeting tomorrow morning and the rules had changed. The physical surroundings were the same, but something was entirely different. No one was defensive or working in overdrive to showcase his or her brilliance. You and your colleagues shared the unvarnished truth because you weren't overly worried about others accepting you, your ideas, or what might happen if you were wrong. The power of ideas won in every case, not the power of politics. Hidden personal agendas were replaced by the business agenda. The thinking was fresh, uncontaminated, and lucid. Speed was balanced with direction, and innovative solutions were tied to the most important needs.

Although that's an image of the ideal business world, it *is* possible, even if it is light years away from the kind of business world we've become accustomed to.

Our unapologetic goal is to change that world, from the inside out. Our pursuit of perfection in the business world is founded on the belief that within each of us is the possibility of perfection.

The Personal Payoff

Whether you are in a staff-level position or are a line manager, a senior executive, or an up-and-coming CEO, if you adopt businessThink you will have the tools you need to become indispensable to your company and deliver the results your company needs. We simply hold out the goal that consistent application of businessThink allows perfection to emerge. If what you do directly contributes to the "perfect world," there are some serious upsides for both you and your company.

Upsides for You
- People value your ideas and insights.
- You trust your intuition and business acumen.
- Colleagues trust your judgment and leadership.
- It opens the door to opportunities you value.
- Your talents are leveraged and utilized.

- Your creativity and perspective open up.
- You become highly influential and relevant.
- You create value.

Upsides for Your Company

- You always evaluate costs against a value proposition.
- Opportunities are seized.
- Problems are prevented early and often, and those that do arise are solved quickly and accurately.
- Shareholders and stakeholders gain confidence.
- Proposed ideas and change meet with optimism.
- Collaboration thrives.
- The company creates and maintains product and service relevance.

When you're finished reading this book, you will be equipped to transform your thinking and the business environment around you.

CHAPTER ONE

Think!

For just a moment, let's transport you back to the radically different corporate scene of 1892. Although there is a revolution happening, this is hardly what we'd expect in our modern world—few lights, no e-mail, no cell phones, no conference rooms, and an economy just shifting from the farm to the factory. As a newly transported businessperson (and therefore unemployed), the only job available is working in a factory for $2 a *day*. Most people, when they walk through the factory doors, are just cogs in a strange new industrial machine: Punch a clock, shut off your brain, turn on your brawn, and hit the factory floor. Managers think, employees lift.

After a few weeks on the job, something peculiar is happening with one of the guys on the factory floor—a shop clerk. He doesn't just show up and do his job like everybody else. On his breaks he grabs a notepad, sometimes even a stopwatch, and starts writing while people work. He intently watches people do their jobs, some days with one group or part of the factory, and other days with someone else in another part of the factory. He records the time it takes to shovel coal, load trains, drill metal, cut patterns, push carts, pull levers—whatever relates to the particular task at hand. After timing each person's tasks down to the second, he then rearranges the tools and tasks they're doing to improve the quality and productivity of their work. Sometimes he asks permission of his peers to do or try something they just did, again, only a little different each time, and even with different tools, some of which he's invented. They aren't quite sure what he's up to, but with a raised eyebrow they oblige.

As time passes he formally introduces himself—Frederick Taylor. You discover he graduated from the Stevens Institute of Technology, a prestigious school, and worked full-time while earning his degree. He comes from a wealthy family, and he's even won today's version of the U.S. Open in tennis doubles. The question on everybody's mind is "What's this guy doing working in a factory for $2 a day?"

After a while, Taylor gets noticed by the owners and is promoted. Now he sets more of his ideas into motion. He begins changing the way everyone and everything works, and they all get more done with the same effort. His processes eliminate piles of wasted iron and devour tons of excess metal scrap. He notices that there are far too many managers and workers for what is being done. Before long the staff is lean, yet the work output continues to improve. Fewer people are sitting around waiting for instructions or work. Inventory isn't stacked too high or too deep like it used to be. Half-finished goods vanish. When you look at all the tremendous results of his actions, you might start to wonder how you could transport this Frederick Taylor dude back to the future where you work.

Although he was a bit fanatical, management loved him because output was up and costs were consistently down. Quality *and* speed were his forte. Every work process was streamlined, tight, and maximized. Taylor changed virtually everything in the factory for the better; every *motion* of work and every *movement* of people improved. It wasn't long before he started his own consulting firm and began working with his first client, Bethlehem Steel. Applying what he learned through his intense curiosity and desire to improve the business world he lived in, he eventually turned Bethlehem Steel into *the* model manufacturing firm. The century's first management consultant (hold on to your wallets) or business guru was born.[1]

Frederick Winslow Taylor was a business revolutionary. Peter Drucker, the modern-day father of management gurus, has called him the most influential person in business of the past 100 years. He discovered rules that changed the productivity of people and improved the profitability of companies, worked toward a more humanistic way to manage, and even invented modern accounting systems while he was at it. Taylor's work allowed the business world to take a giant step forward, and corporations paid attention. He was just a common, ordinary guy with an extraordinary interest and intense curiosity about how work happens. He was also one of the first people to practice some key rules of what we call businessThink. Through a surprisingly simple method of thinking and doing, he maximized work to drive growth and profitability while making his business a better place to work.

Reincarnating Frederick Taylor

Fast-forward to today. The world you work in needs a business-Think revolution. The good news is that you *can* transport the ideas, practices, and spirit of the work of the revered Mr. Taylor to your business world—your office, your company. The first step is to embrace the soul of his intense curiosity about how work really happens. The second step is to find out how you can measure the productivity of those who occupy the sea of cubicles and conference rooms around you and maximize the business. That's no easy task.

Taylor himself would be challenged if he spent a day frantically jotting down notes on his clipboard as he watched people meet, strategize, meet again, analyze risk, e-mail, make calls, meet again, and write memos. He might be able to measure the frenetic activity itself, but he wouldn't learn much from it. As he sat puzzled, his burning questions at the end of his first day of observation might be, "What do businesspeople actually *do?* They *seem* busy. Some people even seem overwhelmed, but what am I going to rearrange to make them more productive? What's the fundamental nature of work here?"

The New Motion and Movement Work

What people *do* is not the equivalent, or the essence, of what makes them *productive* in their work. Guessing what to change in the activities themselves—meetings, e-mails, memos, rearranging people, restructuring organization charts—might provide the illusion of progress, but it wouldn't hold out much hope for better *output,* or even faster output. Output is driven by the activities people engage in: Activity originates with a conscious decision. What people decide to do—fast or not, right or not—is based on the results of their thinking.

> **Stripped down to its essentials, the motion and movement of business *today* is thinking. You get paid to think! That is the new fundamental nature of work.**

It is the crucial, common thread that weaves its way throughout the fabric of every department, team, division, and boardroom. Whether the stakes are big or small; whether the situations are uncommon or routine; whether a decision is strategic or tactical, thinking through what you *could* do, and then deciding what you *should* do, is the essential distinction people have to start making. People may be able to get more efficient by rearranging the activities, but to become more *effective* requires a change in thinking itself. So if thinking is the new fundamental nature of work, how do you measure the success of your work? Well, let's look at the decisions that flow from your thinking, and that may give you the first indication of how productive you are.

The Grand Canyon between Ideas and Results

Dr. Paul Nutt, a professor at Ohio State University's Fischer College of Business, has studied the results that flow from people's decisions. Over the past 19 years, Nutt tracked the success rate of decisions made by executives and managers at 356 different companies. This is what he found: **More than 50 percent of all decisions failed; they were quickly abandoned, only partially implemented, or never adopted at all.**

The rate at which decisions fail is alarming, and those decisions don't fail for only one reason.

- More than 130 decisions reflected an egotistical take-charge approach. Even after the take-charge approach, only 42 percent of those decisions were adopted, and barely a handful of those ended up working.
- When it comes to executives, nearly two-thirds never explored any alternatives once they made up their mind. When options

were offered, they only dug their heels in deeper. Sixty percent of those decisions were dropped, used only in part, or were bombs.

- Eighty-one percent of managers and executives pushed their decisions through by persuasion or edict. Persuasion failed 53 percent of the time, and edict 65 percent. They failed not only because the decisions lacked sound thinking, but because people resented manipulative, heavy-handed tactics, even when the decisions had merit.

- Only 7 percent of the decisions were made after considering long-term priorities or conferring with colleagues.[2]

Surprised? If someone asked *you* how many of *your* business decisions fail or how many of your initiatives collapse, would your answer be "Half"? Ours wouldn't.

If you were asked to rate your confidence as a business decision maker on a scale of 1 to 10, with 1 being "I can't believe someone actually pays me to think" and 10 being "People occasionally worship at the altar of my business brilliance," how would you rate it? Here comes the bizarre, weird twist in contrast to the failure. If you answered somewhere close to "worship" you're right in line with 91 percent of your colleagues worldwide.

In a recent survey, when 818 professionals and managers were asked about their confidence in the quality of their business decisions over the past three years, 91 percent said their confidence had *increased* or stayed the same.[3]

Hmmmm. So in other words, over 50 percent of decisions fail, one way or another, and 91 percent of businesspeople are as confident as ever in their ability to make those decisions. Decision confidence is up. Decision success is down. That is what you might call a gap. Gap is an understatement. It's the Grand Canyon.

We've carefully observed the gap with our own eyes, and it's still hard to believe. In fact, it's pretty surprising, considering how long we've all been doing this business thing, that we're not walking on water by now. Hard to believe or not, half of all decisions fail or don't turn out as projected, and it shows up in the market.

From 1917 to 1987, only 39 members of the original Forbes 100 companies survived. Of those still alive, only two, General Electric and Eastman Kodak, outperformed the market from 1917 to 1987. Only 74 distinguished members of the original Standard & Poor's (S&P) 500 survived to make it to 1997. Only 12 of those survivors (merely 2.4 percent) outperformed the market from 1957 to 1997.[4] Apparently, "standard and poor" is a fitting, and pretty literal, description of S&P's performance. One study revealed that 65 percent of strategic acquisitions and mergers have been failures, resulting in negative shareholder value and market-share. Despite the numbers, merger mania is alive and well.[5] And it's not only the "big muchachos" and traditional businesses that take the hit. The failure figures hold whether it's pre- or post-Internet time, whether it's e-business or brick and mortar, or whatever is invented next.

Roughly 25,000 of the 30,000 e-businesses that had been recently rocking the economic world with initial public offerings (IPOs)—many with nothing more than potential—collapsed.[6] One Small Business Administration study indicated that 60 percent of all new businesses fail within the first six years of operation.[7] Globally, Dun and Bradstreet estimates that 82 percent go under by their tenth anniversary.[8] Some experts estimate that 95 percent of all new products fail.[9] Yesterday the venture capital windows to money heaven were open for a record number of start-ups and IPOs. The windows now appear to be slammed shut.

> The gigantic chasm between ideas and results must be closed by each company and individual. Companies don't get free rides, and we all live and die by what we produce.

"This is the real world, muchachos, and we are all in it."[10]

Mental Flatlining Equals Bad Decisions

Here's just one obituary from the statistics of failed business that shows how we can unnecessarily wipe out an original, hot idea for a business by making a series of bad decisions. The idea was a now-bankrupt grocery delivery service called Webvan. Webvan had great service—the people who delivered orders were polite and knowledgeable, brought the groceries you asked for, and showed up exactly when they said they would (pay attention here, cable companies). It would seem to us that this is how business is supposed to work at its finest. Good prices, great service, and delivery of what you want. If you were a customer, all was right with the world, and you could count on Webvan. Unfortunately, as a shareholder, what you could also count on was the mental flatlining that took place for some key management decisions. A great article written by Stewart Alsop for *Fortune* illustrated the point.[11]

> At a time when Webvan had just two quarters' worth of cash in the bank, the company started repainting all of its brightly colored vans. After less than two years of operations, Webvan decided to launch a rebranding campaign. Rebranding? The company's brand was barely established in the minds of its few customers! The company was running out of money, and raising more money was getting harder every day, yet management decided *to get the vans repainted*. I'm sure the amount was small, perhaps less than $100,000. But that was cash out the door, cash that could never be used for any other purpose. Which illustrates one reason Webvan failed—there were no real entrepreneurs running this company.

Real entrepreneurs never let money out the door for any reason that doesn't strictly advance the business of the company.

My wife and I wish Webvan had spent money on improving the Website rather than on repainting its vans. We wish management had spent that money learning what we wanted from our purchases—had they done so, they could have charged us higher fees for tailored services. We wish they had experimented more with shorter delivery times or larger ordering windows or any other operational changes that would lead to greater efficiency. I wish this wasn't such a sad, sad tale. Webvan management squandered nearly $1 billion of very cheap capital.

Everyone does their fair share of "repainting vans" and mental flatlining. Nobody's perfect. If you look around it's pretty obvious it's not just Webvan—there are hundreds, maybe even thousands, of tragic stories just like theirs. However, you can no longer afford to chalk it up to the traditional, easy verbal escapes—"No pain, no gain," "Thinking outside the box," or "If you're not failing, you're not trying anything new." It's great to keep getting up after each defeat, and we applaud the courage and undying resilience. The truth remains that there are consequences, long-term and short-term, to making bad decisions. It's simply not okay to keep doing the same things over and over again and expecting different results. You have to think more rigorously about what you want to do before you use scarce company resources, and then play "wait and see." In other words, it is more important than ever to *think!*

The Price of Mental Flatlining

Let's skip the comparisons between business and sports that have low averages which make everyone feel better about mistakes that waste resources and get in the way of results: Success in business isn't a good batting average or field-goal percentage or a total of shots on goal or punches landed.

> This is *not* a sport. It's real life. When you're the one on the line to deliver results, the analogies don't offer much comfort. The risks of solutions that don't work are so great that they can affect your very survival and the survival of your company.

The payoff for elevating your thinking is not just survival, but a thriving company and a successful career. The challenge before all of us is that the cold, hard numbers show that there is a monumental gap that separates us from the results we want. Business-people are in trouble and, according to the research, in denial.

The pounding you take from the consistent mental flatlining and the pervasive gap between what you *need* and what you *get* can affect you personally, and can result in something like this:

- People don't want you to think (for yourself or anyone else).
- You start doubting your intuition or business acumen.
- People don't trust your judgment or leadership.
- Flawed thinking costs you money, your position, and career opportunities.
- *You* lose confidence in you, and *others* lose confidence in you.
- Your valuable talents go unused and unrecognized.

- Your creativity and perspective are diminished.
- You are blamed, and often labeled, for not producing results.
- You become critical of others and compare yourself to them.
- If others are making poor decisions, you lose hope.
- You become irrelevant and are no longer needed by your company.
- You leave the company, voluntarily or by invitation.

The price the company pays for collective mental flatlining can be as bad as this:

- Direct costs go up (way up).
- The opportunities the company was hoping to capitalize on are gone.
- The problems the organization was hoping to solve are still hanging around, and maybe they're now bigger.
- Shareholders and clients lose confidence, not to mention the analysts.
- If you are in a management position, the people following you abdicate.
- Proposed ideas are increasingly met with cynicism.
- Change (needed or not) meets with stronger resistance.
- Collaboration dies.
- The best talent in the organization bolts.
- The company becomes irrelevant and goes away.

Needless to say, the price of mental flatlining is high and the reasons for a revolution in businessThinking have serious upsides.

The Secret to White Collar Productivity

While you'll probably never eliminate the risks of failure, or let the fear of failure completely stop you from trying bold, new things (and you shouldn't), what if you could increase the success rate of your ideas from 50 percent to even just 60 percent by changing the "motion and movement" of your thinking?

If we can get results to match the extraordinary level of our confidence, it will make a dramatic difference.

To find the key variable that would make a difference, people for the last 20 years or so have "worried to a frazzle about blue-collar productivity . . . but, truth is, have largely ignored white-collar productivity" (Tom Peters).[12] Because the need for growing white-collar productivity has been largely ignored, the risks of failure haven't changed in decades. White-collar productivity is not immediately quantifiable and as a result is harder to measure because it's not exactly observable in real time (or hasn't been, until now).

Currently, in the white-collar world, the odds for success are squarely on the side of failure. It's up to you to change the odds. In Taylor's words, you need to rearrange and "standardize" your motion and movement in thinking and communicating. In our words, success requires optimizing the thinking of the most amazing technology the business world has access to: human beings.

People have been trained to think in ways that fit the Industrial Age, not the post-Industrial Age. . . . We have to rewire people with new thinking skills
—Gary Hamel[13]

At least one fundamental belief will have to change before the rewiring can begin.

It used to be that in the white- and blue-collar worlds, all rights of thinking were assigned to the boss. It was assumed that he or she (usually he) was the only one with enough management savvy and experience to think, or with enough foresight to set the business agenda, design the strategy, or solve problems. Everyone else carried out the orders like good soldiers. Not anymore.

> **What used to be "somebody else's" job is now *everybody's* job. You have just as much of a responsibility to think as the CEO. If you're the CEO, everyone in your company has just as much responsibility to think as you do. Maybe more!**

Although you may not think of yourself as a businessperson, you *are* a *business*person. All unrivaled, unquestioned business intelligence does not reside in the boardroom. The days of "boss" and "employee," or referring to anyone outside the boardroom as the "rank and file," are quickly being wiped out. Square footage in someone's office, the title on their door, where they get to park, or the size of their salary doesn't entitle anyone to the exclusive rights of business thinking.

The Red Tape Police

> *The painful reality is that many managers, leaders, and companies don't pay people to think—they pay (hope, pray, expect) people to agree—with them!*

To truly enable people to think business there must be a manifest respect for everyone as businesspeople and a standard for doing what is now everyone's responsibility. If everyone is business-Thinking, they are worthy of respect. Without businessThink competence, respect, and accountability, you often end up with the "red tape police" running around the organization, creating additional requirements for the incompetent and unnecessary barricades for the competent. If you can change the way you think, and build a common, optimized approach for unleashing the potential of human technology, you can change the fundamental nature of the work you do and align it for the results you want.

The Default Decision Approach:
Rock, Paper, Scissors

It's scary to think about the failure we've been living with. It's even scarier when you consider that the failure or success of your decisions is also pretty much unpredictable and random! Everyone seems to have their own standards, functional rules, and personal preferences for making decisions.

> Almost 90 percent of businesspeople say there is *no* common approach or common criteria for making decisions where they work.[14]

It's no wonder that the results are also unpredictable and random. In the absence of something—anything—people make up their own rules. The standard can depend on anything: the success of the last decision they made, who they are working with, what they're feeling like on a particular day, the size of the group making the decision, or the political pressure in a specific meeting. Occasionally it feels like the game schoolchildren play called "rock, paper, scissors," where you have a one-third chance of success at each try and there is no way to turn the odds in your favor. Sometimes the approaches people take change the instant a new management book hits the best-seller list. (Yeah, we get the irony of that statement.) Sometimes it works, sometimes it doesn't. The rules for businessThinking will always be relevant.

Rebuilding the ground rules of business starts with a standardized, optimized approach for thinking and communicating. This doesn't mean that we propose blind conformity or mundane generic approaches. What we do mean is to create a unifying theme or common language built specifically for the new motion and movement of the work you do, and to help every single person create *monumental* value, rather than just add *incremental* value or "do their jobs." It is a "conversion kit" to leverage the unique insight and ability of people to make meaningful contributions, and to refine and sharpen business instincts about what will work and what won't. In essence, it is an early litmus test for ideas, decisions, or solutions rather than playing the traditional "wait and see" game. Here are the ground rules for a standardized, optimized approach to getting it right and getting thinking on track.

Eight Rules of businessThink

 1. *Check Your Ego at the Door.*   Arrogance, defensiveness, and the desperate need for approval shut down dialogue, opportunities, and decisions, and end up devouring time and energy, not to mention people. Changing yourself can lead to changing the business.

 2. *Create Curiosity.*   Curiosity is the driving force behind businessThinking, and it thrives on intellectual diversity. Breakthrough solutions require fresh thinking, and curiosity drives your exploration of the unknown. What we currently know can get in the way of the unknown and the pursuit of phenomenal solutions. Your ability to enact curiosity can help create a culture that encourages everyone to ask questions and discourages those who don't.

3. *Move Off the Solution.*   Solutions are only valuable for the results they get, and some solutions get better results than others. Avoid solutions that serve more as distractions than bona fide solutions. Get to the core of underlying business issues that need to be addressed through the desired solution by bringing clarity and definition to the issues, then deciding to focus attention on only the vital few.

4. *Get Evidence.*   If you don't have evidence, there is no reason to do anything—*period!* Get proof that a business problem needs to be solved or that an opportunity *could* exist by collecting soft evidence, and then convert soft evidence into hard evidence that your business can measure.

5. *Calculate the Impact.*   Just because you *can* do something doesn't mean you *should*. It's not unusual that the cost of a solution is more than the cost of living with the problem. Make sure early on that your investment has a worthwhile impact on the company, and solid economic return. You'll never know unless you convert hard evidence into money. Converting hard evidence into money will help you make the move from the subjective to the objective, and from the could to the should.

6. *Explore the Ripple Effect.*   By widening your functional lens to capture the broader impact of problems or opportunities on the company, you are calculating more than financial impact. Make sure you know who or what else in the company is affected to get the full scope of impact. Move beyond functional silos, cubicle walls, and organization chart structures.

7. *Slow Down for Yellow Lights.*   There are hurdles that can stop any solution dead in its tracks. If the problem or opportunity is as big as you think it is, what has stopped everyone from successfully doing something about it before now? What (or who) might stop you in the future?

8. *Find the Cause.*   Dig for the underlying reason the symptoms of your problem are showing up. Make sure you're treating the cause of the problem rather than the effects. Ask why.

Emotional and Intellectual Fusion

The ground rules begin and end with the one primary tool you will need—your mind. The rules for revolutionizing businessThinking rely on your emotional intelligence and intellectual "horsepower." Raw intellect—your intelligence quotient (IQ)—is a measure of how head-smart you are. Raw emotional intelligence—your emotional quotient (EQ)—is a measure of how emotionally smart and self-aware you are. businessThink brilliance requires fusing EQ and IQ and elevating their performance. Unfortunately, each trait has a superiority complex. IQ says, "I'm so smart (and you are ruled by your emotions)," while EQ fires back, "You might be smart, but you don't understand people (you have no social skills)." For business-Think, you need to elevate both sides and fuse them together.

EQ: The Good, the Bad, and the Ugly

Business is largely about communication and collaboration, and that makes emotional intelligence vital. This might sound boring and tired—but it's just true. Emotional intelligence is partly your ability to trust your instincts and emotions, even to the point of overriding the input your intellect may have provided. High business EQ is a measure of how effectively and quickly you can talk openly, human being to human being, and open beliefs to discussion. High EQ brings the maturity and willingness to clarify and test assumptions, presuppositions, and mental models.

Ignoring IQ (or in its absence), some people rely on EQ exclusively and intuit their way to decisions. Occasionally, regardless of all the data dredged up by due diligence, making the best business decisions requires finely tuned intuition. When decisions based on only intuition work out for the best, you're nigh unto a deity. While you may not admit it outwardly, all you can say is, "I just went with my gut feel."

> *The danger of using an exclusively intuitive approach to business is that you can be highly susceptible to blind spots.*

Max Bazerman of the Kellogg Graduate School of Management obviously isn't too high on the exclusively intuitive approach, as he said in *Fast Company:* "Often, when you hear about intuition, what you're really hearing is a justification of luck. Intuition will lead you astray; it's drastically overrated."[15] Your hunches are usually better when they are informed and evaluated by intellect.

EQ Isolation: Kum-bay-ya

We've worked for companies that were much higher in emotional intelligence than intellect. One in particular was an international firm that had an incredible ability to develop rapport with clients. As a result, clients openly and willingly shared a great deal of information about their problems. The company was able to help clients understand their problems better than the clients could by themselves, and clients entered these engagements with unbridled enthusiasm. At the end of the firm's prepackaged interventions, everyone wanted to join hands and sing "Kum-bay-ya," but the long-term refrain was a chorus of disappointment.

Even with EQ that was off the charts, the company lacked the intellectual horsepower to take what they learned from the clients about their problems, link it to the right solution, and deliver sound business results. Consequently, they often resorted to off-the-shelf, cellophane-wrapped solutions. When the canned solutions worked, it was luck. When they didn't, it was hard luck.

> **Luck is not a method.**

The unpredictability was a big disappointment to their clients, and was a serious limitation to their own growth.

IQ: Intellectual Horsepower

In *business,* IQ is a measure of how effectively you can pull together information and synthesize data to make meaningful decisions—how much intellectual rigor you can apply to your analysis. Intellect helps you balance your gut instinct with data, gather evidence and impact for key issues, uncover critical constraints, apply good tenets of systemic thinking, and carefully explore implications of one idea on the whole. In essence, it's the willingness to take a detached, unbiased view of what is really going on.

> *The majority of businesses [people] are incapable*
> *of original thought because they are unable*
> *to escape from the tyranny of reason.*
> —David Ogilvy, Ogilvy and Mather

Sometimes when you rely exclusively on "just the facts"—the percentages, the information that flows from due diligence, and the isolated left-brained analysis of cold, hard data—occasionally it's just what the business needs. It's also often incomplete, stifling, and emotionally lazy.

IQ Isolation: Beware the Piranha

We once worked with one of the world's top strategy firms. They ate, drank, and slept IQ, almost exclusively. When someone threw an idea on the table in meetings, it was like watching piranha feed. People attacked and devoured the idea, tore it apart, and if anything was left after the feeding frenzy, people said, "Oh, it must be a good idea." For some it was a workable form of critical thinking, although not without casualties internally. We often observed many good ideas getting held back for fear of being eaten alive!

The problem worsened when they tried to use the "piranha process" with clients, who found it to be tremendously arrogant and intimidating. Many clients described the consultants as "brains on a stick." Clients put up with them for two or three weeks, occasionally even for two or three months, but rarely for two or three years. Many quit doing business with them. The strategy firm had to significantly stretch and focus on a balance of emotional and intellectual energy to recover as a business.

The fusion of EQ and IQ should be so tight, the weld so strong, that it deserves a new Q (Figure 1.1). Elevating EQ and IQ and blending them together equals the *X quotient* (XQ)—the ability to access and utilize both forms of intelligence as you think and collaborate in business. XQ gives you the ability to ask hard questions in a soft way. If you're going to get high-powered thinking and better decisions, ask some tough questions—questions to which a

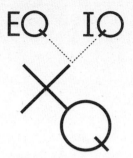

Figure 1.1 EQ + IQ = XQ.

little voice in your brain often says, "Oh, you can't ask that. That's too hard! That would offend them." XQ will allow you to know which hard questions need to be asked, and in a way that builds rapport. By not asking at all, you miss the discovery of vital information that is crucial to success. Get ready to elevate your XQ and to live the new rules of businessThink.

Check Your Ego
at the Door

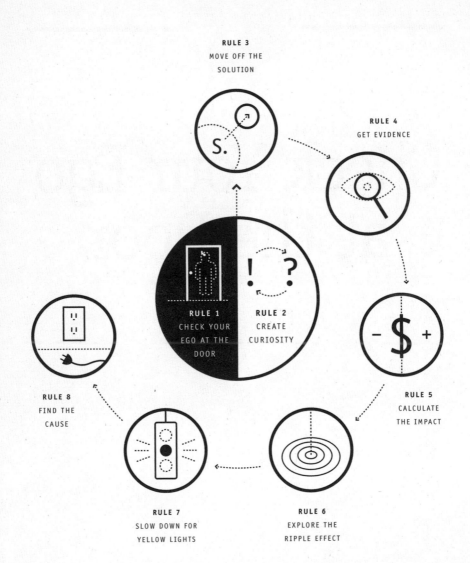

RULE 3
MOVE OFF THE
SOLUTION

RULE 4
GET EVIDENCE

S.

RULE 1
CHECK YOUR
EGO AT THE
DOOR

RULE 2
CREATE
CURIOSITY

RULE 8
FIND THE
CAUSE

RULE 5
CALCULATE
THE IMPACT

RULE 7
SLOW DOWN FOR
YELLOW LIGHTS

RULE 6
EXPLORE THE
RIPPLE EFFECT

− $ +

Many believe that ego is indispensable in order to survive in the ruthless, unforgiving business world. It's not unusual to see businesspeople operating on ideas like "Eat or be eaten," "Do or die," and "Step on anyone in your way." Success seems to be the entitlement that only the aggressive enjoy; in business, bravado inherits the earth.

In direct contrast to those beliefs, the one thing we see that shuts down people, and companies, more than anything else is ego. We're not talking about the healthy kind of ego.

> Our working definition of ego is not personal confidence, self-assuredness, or self-awareness. Contrary to what owners of ego may think, ego is not equivalent to strength. Ego masquerades as confidence, but is quickly and easily recognized by others as insecurity and arrogance.

Arrogance consumes everything and everyone in its path. Ego has no pleasure other than in superiority over others—their ideas, worth, position, and value. Likewise, egotism plays the zero-sum game and shuts out possibility. Ego relentlessly seeks comparison, and gains satisfaction only by having more than another. Ego is under the delusion it is always right because it pretends to know everything, especially more than anyone else.

Nobody knows *everything* they need to know to make crucial decisions in something as complex as business. Making the right decision requires important information and clear thinking from colleagues. You can't get relevant information or the best thinking from colleagues if they check out when they're crowded out by your arrogance, defensiveness, or fear. And if you get less relevant information, and only the thinking that helps everyone feel safe, your potential to succeed will be shut down.

Checking Your Ego at the Door will give you the tools to create an environment that cultivates open business dialogue rather than shutting it down. You will know how to unite ideas and people rather than polarize them, and create understanding rather than confusion. Dialogue will be balanced with both open communication and critical thinking, expanding rather than restricting possibilities.

• CHAPTER TWO •

Ego Alert!

About 10 years ago, I (Steve) started my own company with some partners. After about two years of acting out the entrepreneurial dream, things weren't exactly going according to plan. We were cash-strapped. Many of us were carrying heavy credit card debt that would make any bank shareholder proud. In the early days, credit was our only source of early capital. When a new credit card application came in the mail, we jumped for joy—we had another "venture capital partner." Our nonplastic investors were supportive during that time, but were growing anxious.

We were humble enough to ask for advice then. We called people from our Rolodexes who were respected business leaders and educators and held a meeting, with the guests serving as our board of advisors. There were about 13 people there; most were general managers, educators, and presidents of multi-million-dollar organizations. We spent the entire evening feeding the advisors ideas, asking for feedback, and getting their opinions. We worked the room as best we could to keep the advisors' egos in check as each advisor passionately gave their point of view. Many suggested that the company's offering was too vague, and that we as partners were underqualified to deliver what we said we could deliver. The advisors suggested we stay with the basics, keep it simple until we had more capital and experience, and then raise the complexity of our offering.

The Ego Has Landed

I remember the ride home with my partners in my crowded Volkswagen bug (the car of choice for young entrepreneurs who are broke). We carefully reviewed the feedback we'd gathered, considered what each person had to say, and then handily dismissed the group of advisors as a bunch of old guys who were out of touch with the market. We found special causes to dismiss the advisors' feedback; we categorized most of it as "not progressive" or "not visionary." We had mortgaged our lives, not to mention our hopes, to make this work, and we wanted to do what we thought was innovative and cutting edge. A little over two years later, after going against the ideas the advisors had suggested would bring success, we were out of business. The partnership was just one more corporate crash that showed up as a statistic in the graveyard of ego-driven casualties.

In the end, the feedback the advisors gave us was valid; we just couldn't hear it—maybe because it was very *real*. It was hard to think (and listen), considering the personal risk and debt we each carried with us to every sales appointment and board meeting. It was challenging to listen to anything beyond our personal determination and outside of what was generated by the sheer force of our will. To admit we were wrong, or to admit an early defeat, was simply out of the question. To simplify what we were offering seemed pedestrian to us.

It wasn't long before the suggestions that came out of the advisory session were in the rearview mirror of our emotional and intellectual reach. Nothing could stop our undoing, not even business school lessons. The business classes we took did little to save us. We knew all the technical information we needed to know. Although we thought we had a phenomenal idea, we had no hard evidence to prove that the market valued what we had to offer. We had great ideas, the beginnings of an innovative brand, and the resolve to make it work, but it was our egos that took us down. We wanted to demonstrate our brilliance to the world, and all the while held defensively to what we thought should work. We ended up on the bleeding edge, not the leading edge.

According to Dr. Paul Nutt's research, over one-third of all decisions reflect an egotistical take-charge approach. Even with the take-charge approach, only 42 percent of decisions are adopted, and barely a handful of those end up working. When it comes to executives, nearly two-thirds never explore any alternatives once they make up their mind, even when alternatives are offered. Sixty percent of those decisions are dropped, used only in part, or are bombs.[1] In the end, we had bombed.

The Achilles Heel of Strength

We learned the hard way that the very traits you count as strengths can turn into weaknesses. When we started our company we tried to hire the best we could find. We were absolutely passionate about our work, and driven to make the company succeed. Each founder and employee had unique abilities and strengths, and yet something got in the way. One of the partners once mentioned that we might be letting our egos get in the way, but we dropped the discussion in favor of our own ideas. That's where the danger lies. Unless there is finely tuned self-awareness, ego is easily overdeveloped, even if imperceptibly.

> Without a heightened awareness of the development of your own ego, healthy characteristics and unique, powerful talents can become destructive and degenerate into weakness.

This Strength . . .	. . . When Multiplied by Ego Breeds:
Confidence	A sense of infallibility
Quickness	Overhastiness
Sharp wit	Abrasiveness
Alertness	Narrow focus
Dedication	Workaholism
Control	Inflexibility
Courage	Foolhardiness
Perseverance	Resistance to change
Charm	Manipulation
Ambition	Coercion
Power	Autocracy
Flexibility	Ambivalence

Source: Adapted from John R. O'Neil, *The Paradox of Success* (Los Angeles: J. P. Tarcher, 1994), p. 67.

Got Ego?

Even with the best of intentions, talents, gifts, confidence, aspirations, and ambition sometimes mutate into overconfidence, arrogance, and overzealousness, and eventually transmute into a huge ego. The problem, however, may be subtle and hard to detect. In many ways, Jack Welch, the former CEO of General Electric, could be considered the premier businessThinking CEO of our time. And just because he is a great businessThinker now doesn't mean it was easy getting there, or that he did it perfectly along the way. In his book, *Jack: Straight from the Gut,* he points out that the biggest mistake he made while at GE was when he was "just full of [him]self" and decided to acquire Kidder Peabody, then one of Wall Street's oldest and premier investment banking firms.[2] Counter to the experience and advice of two of his most trusted and experienced directors, who knew the financial industry better than he did, his ego crept in, causing him to think that he could make anything work. Because of illegal insider trading that had occurred before GE acquired Kidder Peabody, the acquisition was a disaster. GE ended up being saddled with $26 million in fines, and later losses amounted to a $350 million disaster that sucked money from every division's profits. Personally, it was one of Welch's darkest hours.

How do you know if *you* have an ego to shut down?

The truth is, we all can stand to control our egos. If you're breathing, that's your first sign that you have an ego. Ego is a difficult thing to nail down because it requires carefully paying attention to your responses and those of others. The challenge is that ego is not like a machine that can simply be physically opened up and fixed; it's mental and emotional machinery that has to be taken apart and tuned up.

To compound the complexity of ego, people who have the biggest problems with it often don't think they have a problem with ego. While they may or may not be addicted to ego, they also don't recognize the signs when they're a little doped up.

Here are some key warning signs we've noticed that indicate someone is in the "ego zone":

- You are showcasing your brilliance.
- You are constantly seeking approval from others.
- You are being defensive.

Specific responses are as different as individual personalities. The broad warning shot across the bow is if you feel yourself exhibiting one of the preceding signs (or you believe you are one of the most humble people you know).

The Cloud of Self-Absorption

When *showcasing your brilliance,* ironically, you lose credibility. Your brilliance, if it *really* exists, is lost in the cloud of your self-absorption. People stop seeing the brilliance, and notice only the arrogance. People get more hung up on your demonstrations than they do on the strengths and weaknesses of your ideas. The sad thing is that even when the thinking is really brilliant, people ignore it because they want to shut *you* down.

> *Most people are anxious to accept ideas that are "good" by down-to-earth people rather than get beaten over the head by the stone tablets after someone's pretentious walk down the mountain of "Me, Myself, and I."*

When your ego is revved up, there's a natural tendency to nose-dive into the deep (so you think) recesses of your brilliance when someone identifies a business concern. You think to yourself, "I'm a mile ahead of them. They need my expertise. I'll weave my magic and fix them." You quickly formulate some response (usually a lecture) while they are talking to you (which means you are not listening), and as soon as they take a breath you jump in and start telling them what you think they need. We are all guilty of having done this at some time (or many times). As you listen to the words of your own suggestions, your internal smile widens as you acknowledge how (b)right you are. You got brilliance, baby, and if you haven't dazzled them with your genius yet, there's more where that came from!

> Yeah, I called her up, she gave me a bunch of crap about me not listening to her or something. I don't know, I wasn't really paying attention.
>
> **—HARRY, IN THE MOVIE *DUMB AND DUMBER***

Are you giving good advice when you stuff them with your self-defined brilliance? Who knows, if all you do is tell your colleagues what they should do? Showcasing your brilliance carries with it the risk of serious downsides:

- You may be wrong. (It's at least a statistical possibility.)
- People may see you as arrogant.
- You may get no buy-in or ownership from others—which could ensure failure.
- You may get the blame if your idea or suggestion fails.
- Your team may talk only about the ideas you tell them about—and potentially leave many ideas on the table, unexplored.
- You start treating people like things and become efficient rather than effective with other human beings.
- If team members don't shut down entirely, they may start telling you only what you want to hear.

Desperately Seeking Approval

When you're constantly *seeking approval,* you share ideas with the intent of being accepted, liked, and popular—rarely with the intent of inviting a close, hard look at your ideas. When you see or hear thinking that doesn't make sense, or if you see a better way, you're hesitant to share your perspective because you're too worried about what someone else will think of you. If you do speak up, your self-concept is so wrapped up in getting acceptance that if the idea is accepted, you feel accepted. And if it is rejected, you feel personally rejected.

> *With the ego-generated need for approval,*
> *you don't give the unvarnished truth,*
> *explore failure paths, or give your insider's*
> *perspective, often when it's needed most.*

You give people what they *want* to hear, not what they *need* to hear. Basically, you just accept whatever the wind is blowing around as long as approval of you is the outcome. This is how yes-men and yes-women got their infamous start. There's often not much of a difference between an approval-seeking person and an obedient dog or a well-trained parrot. You may argue that simply accepting and obeying may be appropriate. What could possibly go wrong?

- The ideas you blindly follow could be wrong (and you will still be blamed).
- You aren't adding any value—any thought leadership.
- You could leave many opportunities uncovered.
- You could lose the respect of those who do courageously share their perspective, and the respect of those who need your opinion.
- You could get labeled. (We won't go into the labels—but you can use your imagination.)

> **If people are too intimidated or too reluctant to help their leaders lead, their leaders will fail.**
>
> **—MICHAEL USEEM[3]**

Defensive Overdrive

When you're defensive, you don't treat your ideas as testable hypotheses, but as facts to be secured and validated. You dig for evidence with the intent of *proving* your point rather than *discovering* the point.

> *We are most likely to face resistance and counterattack when we enter a conversation afflicted with the deadly disease of certainty. (Of this we're damn certain.)*
> —Patterson, Grenny, McMillan, and Switzler,
> *Better Than Duct Tape*[4]

Instead of asking other people, you ask yourself. When you do ask others, and their answers don't jive with yours, you discount their answers as somehow insufficient or not applicable, or you find some special cause that makes it irrelevant. To give up on your idea or viewpoint would be a major sign of weakness. You listen, but you resist what you hear. What are some of the downsides when you get defensive?

- You don't get critical input to make ideas better.
- You repeat the same mistakes.
- People shut down around you, and leave you isolated.
- You create defensiveness and divisiveness in others.
- Attention is inappropriately shifted from the important issues at hand to people and their positions.

James Dyson is the poster child of a businessThinking entrepreneur, and a businessperson who keeps his ego checked. Not far behind Richard Branson of the Virgin empire (Virgin Airlines, Virgin Records, etc.), Dyson is probably the best known businessperson in Britain. His vacuum cleaner patents have generated over £12 billion in worldwide sales. In his pursuit of perfection, he made more than 5,000 vacuum cleaner prototypes before he launched his final vacuum cleaner (intellectual trial and error at its finest). Now, the biggest vacuum brands such as Hoover and Eureka are paying attention to Dyson.

Given his wild success and determined, entrepreneurial spirit, he remains a person who keeps his ego checked in the pursuit of continuous learning. One of Dyson's colleagues says of him, "I can tell him if I don't agree with him about something. He's prepared to take advice and to change his mind. Many people when they get to that age are inflexible, but not James."

It's not so much age that inflates ego, but our attitude about what we think we know and what we're willing to stay open to. Sometimes it's our past and current success that closes us down. On retiring from the company, Dyson said, "There are a lot of engineers and scientists driving things forward. So, in that sense, I don't think I'll be missed very much. I mean, it's not a one-man business by any stretch."[5] Humble people tend not to be "me-centric" but "us-centric."

The Trust Alarm

If you are showcasing your brilliance, seeking approval, or being defensive, people may feel it, even if you disguise it with well-crafted technique (unless, of course, their own egos are suffocating their senses). People can intuitively sense your intent, and you can sense theirs. There's biology to back this up. On the back of your brainstem is something called the *amygdala*. The amygdala is the part of the mind that serves as the emotional "traffic cop" to quickly determine what's safe and what's not. When people were hunters and gatherers, it worked to make sure that when they needed to run from danger, freeze, or defend themselves, they quickly did so. The amygdala often tells you to do things (or not) before the more advanced part of your brain, the *neocortex,* has a chance to examine them carefully and determine whether they're "safe." In other words, everyone has a built-in BS detector or "trust alarm," and it tells you in an instant when to trust and when not to trust. Have you ever sensed, even after a split-second's first impression, that someone is not to be trusted? Ever seen someone walk into a room, and you can *feel* their ego before they *say* a word? If you have sensed it in *others* in the past, others sense it in *you,* too. They will know if *you* have hidden agendas, if *you're* closed, defensive, and arrogant.

When the ego alarm goes off, dialogue about the business issues quickly turns into a monologue of personal issues. Ego then holds ideas and information hostage, and that becomes the crux of the problem. Instead of fresh, clear, uncontaminated businessThinking, you run into verbal, mental, and emotional stop signs designed to validate ego. Ego defense mechanisms affect ideas and communication in at least four ways. Ego will:

1. *Magnify.* Ego amplifies information beyond its intended significance or meaning.

2. *Filter.* Ego selectively allows in only what validates your own thinking and experience. You also tend to conveniently discard information that is contrary to your position.

3. *Alter.* Ego bends or manipulates information that comes in to support your own ideas or to validate your position.

4. *Fabricate.* Ego creates information that never existed.[6]

When defense mechanisms are in play, people on both sides close down and pump up their own egos. The battle cry is sounded, and people parade their egos to the battlefield, ready for war. When egos clash, any battlefield will do. In the theatre of an ego war, someone proposes a solution that *they* think is right, with the weapon of an exclamation point. Rather than finding a solution, working the system to win others over to their point of view is now a decisive victory. Lines are drawn, sides are taken, and positional and political encampment quickly takes hold. Any discussion about alternatives is now interpreted as conflict, dissension, or rebellion. Challenges to any idea are seen as personal threats. Due diligence becomes ego-serving and biased. People egomaniacally look to see what they want to see, and see only what they look for. Finding only what they want to find, they clench their fists and say, "Yes! I knew I was right. I love being right!"

> **Bad decisions are made because ... emotions like anxiety, greed, exasperation, intolerance, apathy, or fear have hijacked their brains and directed them to the "easy way out," the "path of least resistance," the "safe route," or the "taking care of number one."**
>
> **–ANNETTE SIMMONS, FOUNDER,**
> **GROUP PROCESS CONSULTING, *THE STORY FACTOR*[7]**

Upon arrival at the untested, self-validated idea, they barricade themselves in. Sabers are rattled. Positional power is abused. Decibels climb. Tempers flare. People fight, run, subvert, defend, resist, lobby, or complain—and they lose. They either take the hill or die trying. The casualties are the people they work with, not to mention the business—but who cares: It was a personal victory. Openness is feigned while hearts and minds remain closed.

businessThinking demands open, honest dialogue to balance what's missing in each individual's thinking. Nothing closes down *real* dialogue faster than ego.

Create an environment where ego doesn't feel welcome hanging around. How will you make it safe for ideas to be explored and opened for candid examination, and not be interrupted by ego? The biggest, boldest move is by changing yourself and skillfully using the tool of language.

The businessThink Mirror

In the following test, read each statement and check the box that best describes you. Be honest with yourself; no one's looking. Even though the statements are focused specifically on you, ask the same questions of your department, division, management or executive team, and company. (And if you score perfectly on every question, chances are you may be delusional.)

The businessThink Ego Test

	No	Sometimes	Ego alert
1. When someone is giving me constructive feedback, I get defensive.	❑	❑	❑
2. I often interrupt people because their point is irrelevant or inferior.	❑	❑	❑
3. I get (uptight, nervous, intimidated) when I'm around people who are in more powerful positions or who are above me in the organization.	❑	❑	❑
4. I'm afraid to share candid thoughts and opinions for fear that others may not agree with or accept me.	❑	❑	❑
5. I spend much more time talking than listening.	❑	❑	❑
6. I view the people I report to as my bosses and people who report to me as my employees, rather than my colleagues.	❑	❑	❑
7. When someone challenges my ideas, I tend to take it personally.	❑	❑	❑
8. I am surprised when people don't agree with me.	❑	❑	❑
9. I solicit feedback from others with the intent and expectation of hearing them talk favorably about me.	❑	❑	❑

CHAPTER THREE

The Language of Humility

The H Word

The cure for ego is humility—the big H word. Contrary to popular belief, humility is not weakness. In fact, by our definition, humility is incredibly powerful. It is quiet strength and genuine confidence, tempered with graciousness. It is we-centric, not me-centric, and deflects attention and credit rather than desperately grasping for it. Humility quietly and consistently produces extraordinary results, and focuses on the future for a cause larger than self.

> In contrast to the very I-centric style of comparison leaders, we were struck by how the good-to-great leaders didn't talk about themselves. [Great] leaders channel their ego needs away from themselves and into the larger goal of building a great company.
>
> **–JIM COLLINS, _GOOD TO GREAT_**[1]

Humility adopts the principle of ignorance: "Nobody knows everything about anything." You don't. Don't pretend you do. Neither does anyone else. All of us may know a lot about some things, but we don't know everything about anything. That's why you desperately need collaboration. You may be especially gifted;

we hope you'll eventually be renowned for your talents. But first you have to blend your brilliance with the principle of ignorance and humility. Speaking about the principles of ego and humility in interactions with others, here's what Benjamin Franklin said (this is a mondo quote, but worth the read):

> I make it a rule to forbear all direct contradictions to the sentiments of others, and all positive assertion of my own. I even forbad myself the use of every word or expression in the language that imported a fix'd opinion, such as certainly, undoubtedly, etc., and I adopted instead of them, I conceive, I apprehend, or I imagined a thing to be so or so; or it so appears to me at present. When another asserted something that I thought an error, I deny'd myself the pleasure of contradicting him abruptly, and of showing immediately some absurdity in his proposition: and in answering I began by observing that in certain cases or circumstances his opinion would be right, but in the present case there appear'd or seem'd to me some difference, etc. I soon found the advantage of this change in my manner; the conversations I engaged in went on more pleasantly. The modest way in which I propos'd my opinions procur'd them a readier reception and less contradiction; I had less mortification when I was found to be in the wrong, and I more easily prevail'd with others to give up their mistakes and join with me when I happened to be in the right. And this mode, which I at first put on with some violence to natural inclination, became at length so easy, and so habitual to me, that perhaps for these fifty years past no one has ever heard a dogmatical expression escape me.[2]

Mirror, Mirror, on the Wall

In your pursuit of humility, seek *other-awareness*. You can't be your only barometer of whether you're humble—you need others to be your mirror. Remember, people who have a problem with ego often don't think *they* have a problem. You need someone you trust to "hold up the mirror"; someone who's placed their head on your ego's guillotine before, lived to tell about it, and is still willing to give you the unvarnished truth. When you seek other-awareness, and others give you feedback, it's easy to become defensive. When your reaction is defensive, people regret having given it. If they initiate giving you feedback, even if they are trying to help you in a constructive way, you choose to take it as a personal bullet, and miss the point.

> *Over the past 10 years, we have surveyed over 150,000 managers and professionals, from over 500 companies, including 83 of the Fortune 100. We asked them to rate each other, and themselves, on 78 items of effectiveness in business. The two items that have ranked dead last over more than a decade of asking are "Receives negative feedback without becoming defensive" and "Seeks feedback on ways he/she can improve."*
> —FranklinCovey 360 Research[3]

Down deep inside we're afraid of feedback, and when we do get it, we emotionally or intellectually decapitate the person for sharing it. Sometimes we feign interest, and fake the person out by nodding our heads and pretending we're interested, but it really just ticks us off, and we do nothing about it or quickly forget it. When Roman senators addressed the masses, they had underlings whose sole job was to stand behind them and whisper repeatedly, "Remember, you're mortal." You are, too, and we all need someone to remind us—frequently. If you can remind yourself you're mortal, or be reminded by others, it will make it much easier to swallow your pride or eat healthy portions of crow when necessary.

Don't Feed the Ego

If dealing with ego meant dealing only with your own, it would make the task a lot easier. Dealing with the egos of others is a reality, and can be equally difficult. The best way to manage another person's ego is *not* to feed it. For some reason many people tend to believe that if you just stroke someone's ego, it will go away. We disagree.

> People with ego want their ego fed, and the bigger the portions the better. The stroking only serves to make the appetite more insatiable and dysfunctional. Don't feed the beast.

Deal with their ego through the absence of your own. This doesn't mean you back down and acquiesce. It requires genuine confidence and a sincere regard for the person you're working with. You will need to create an environment of respect through language that neutralizes ego and encourages thoughtful examination of beliefs and positions.

Neutralize Ego

The language begins with a "softening" lead-in statement that invites everyone to drop the figurative boxing gloves. It demonstrates your intent to create a neutral, safe place that removes egotistical responses. You are soft in how you deliver what you say, while remaining direct and clear. This allows you to deal with the person in front of you kindly, directly, and with due respect, while simultaneously getting real on the issues at hand. Start first with what the other person said, and explore it together. Don't go point-counterpoint with them or dazzle them with superior logic and brilliance. Here are some examples of softening statements that we will build into businessThink language:

- I appreciate your asking. When you say. . . .
- Thanks for bringing that up. Could I ask you. . . .
- I hadn't even thought of that. If I could, let me ask you. . . .
- I'd like to answer that. Can you help me out by. . . .
- Good point. Do you mind me asking. . . .
- How big *is* your head? (Just seeing if you were paying attention.)

Years ago, I (Steve) walked into the office of the president and CEO of a potential client. Although people from my company had been meeting with him for some time, this was my first meeting with him. Upon entering his office, he looked up from his desk and said, "What the hell is a young guy like you supposed to teach *me* about my company?" I could hear my ego banging on the door: "*Let me at him!*" But what I said was, "Well, you've been talking with Larry (our salesperson) for a few weeks. Given what I know, I imagine there's a lot you could teach me. However, if there *were* something I *could* teach you relative to what you've been talking about, what would it be?"

This didn't totally check the client's ego, but it did at least sidetrack it long enough that we could have a reasonable, open, candid conversation. Unfortunately, his humility was temporary, and he dismissed anything our research or his employees had to say. Some people spend a lot of money and time to convince themselves they're open, as long as they don't have to actually do anything with what they hear. They fool themselves and hurt their companies.

Softening statements can at least open the door for dialogue, but that doesn't mean ego is permanently checked. When ego comes back in covertly, these are some of the signs that let you know it's in the room.

Search for Missing Comparisons

People often share how they feel without any comparison to something else that people can measure it against. Belief is taken to an extreme, and often punctuated with ego-driven phrases like *too much, too many, too little, too slow, too expensive, better than, worse than.* To businessThink, what you want to know is, *compared to what?* Consider the following scenario:

Colleague: Consolidating all of our vendors, and eliminating some, is way too complicated. We can't do it.

Old School: Have you ever done this before? It's actually not that complicated. If we simply benchmark the competition, according to the research, we will be able to reduce our cost while maintaining . . . blah, blah, blah . . . and in my experience . . . yada, yada, yada.

businessThink: If it is too complicated, that's probably not a good thing [softening statement]. What specifically seems to be the most complicated? Compared to what [your test for the missing comparison]?

The softening statement acknowledges their concern regarding how complicated things could be. You have not agreed it will be (or is) complicated. You also have not taken an opposing position. You're simply asking them to fill in the missing comparison. Then ask them what would solve it to their satisfaction, and invite them to explore the upsides if in fact you were able to resolve the complications.

Uncover Belief Blankets

People can share a belief that covers (or smothers) virtually everything:

- *They* never believe me.
- *Performance* is not rewarded here.
- *Management* ignores us.
- The *market* has no faith in us.

The belief may be real in the mind of the person saying it, but that doesn't necessarily mean it's true. To businessThink, you want to uncover the specifics left out of their statement.

Colleague: Our performance incentive program is a joke. Performance is never rewarded here.

Old School: I think we actually do a pretty good job of rewarding performance. It just has to be the right performance. I don't think they are ignoring your performance as much as you think. Maybe you just need to focus on the real. . . .

businessThink: If your performance isn't being rewarded, that needs to change. Out of curiosity, which performance isn't rewarded? For which things, specifically?

Don't Buy into Black *or* White

People often think in black or white: It's either this or that, go or no-go; if this, then that. The only thing missing is—every other possibility on the planet! To businessThink, you'll ask them to explore other options.

Colleague: This is a marketing issue, not a sales issue. We are *either* going to improve product quality and upgrade our services, *or* we'll have to move to compete on price.

Old School: Well, what you don't understand is that product quality doesn't matter to customers in this market. Besides, our customer satisfaction index is blah, blah, blah. . . .

businessThink: Those may be our only two options; that may make sense. Let's start with your definition of quality (or competing on price).

Beware Absolutes

Sometimes people will share their belief in the language of absolutes: *all, every, never, no one, everyone.* To businessThink, you'll need to explore the exceptions. For example, imagine you're in a call-center meeting talking about the latest customer satisfaction survey, and during the discussion someone says something like this:

Colleague: Every one of our customers is screaming for us to be on the Web. If they can't shop online, our sales will take a dive. I've told them a thousand times, but they never listen.

Old School: Idiots. I totally agree with you. They are so out of touch with what this company really needs.

businessThink: I've wondered about that myself. What would they have to be looking at that would lead them to ignore this kind of data? What kind of information could we get together that would give such a compelling business case that it would get them to pay attention?

Pain Frame versus Gain Frame

When someone proposes a solution, people will often tell you what they don't like about it—what won't work, why something is bad, or why you can't do it that way. They're planting a big stop sign in the middle of the road. While it may be helpful to take a look at what's wrong, it's not helpful when they can't move out of the *pain frame* long enough to see what's possible to prevent it. The language of pain tends to stop discussion; it freezes examination and limits thinking about possibilities.

On the opposite side is the *gain frame*. People stuck here are often optimists, and deal only in possibilities and positives. This sometimes leads to an inability to assess what is really going on today, and where the problems are that need to be addressed. So while they may be upbeat and optimistic and have great vision, this attitude can also freeze examination and restrict an honest, real assessment.

To businessThink, let's combine both frames and call it the *reality frame*. If someone asks whether the glass is half-empty or half-full, businessThink answers: *It's both!* Let's not look exclusively through one frame or the other. In creating the right exploratory environment for both, invite people to consider upsides *and* downsides—the pain *and* the gain. In this case, yielding the right of way to their "frame" is validating, and then examining the opposite side or frame opens them up to other alternatives. This allows them to keep all the upsides they like, and reduce or possibly eliminate the downsides.

Colleague: I absolutely don't like the idea of expanding globally when we're still in chaos domestically. It makes no sense whatsoever.

Old School: Before we go much further, let me show you all the research our cross-functional team did that went into this before we came to that conclusion. We first looked at . . . yada, yada, yada.

In this example, they seem to have experienced something that caused them to make a statement as if it were fact, and this usually comes packed with emotion and ego. But you don't know if the belief behind the statement is accurate and complete, so you businessThink to explore the experience that led to their position.

businessThink: That may well be an important issue that would keep us from expanding. What specifically makes no sense? Let's imagine we weren't in chaos—what would you want instead? What would have to happen before you'd be comfortable moving forward?

When language is used as a weapon of ego, you can use language as a tool to move beyond the barriers ego tries to create. The next time you're in a meeting, on a conference call, or at a strategy session, listen carefully to the language. Make sure you have checked your own ego at the door. As a matter of fact, don't merely check it at the door, because it could still sneak back in. Check it, as in hockey—hard, against the boards—take the two-minute penalty if you have to. When you hear ego, deal with it tactfully and gracefully. Neutralizing ego and exploring options will give you and your company a chance to come up with the best solutions, not just the ones that are possible because you can't get beyond the dysfunction of ego. Solutions that create superb business results require moving beyond ego, so embrace humility!

The businessThink Mirror

In the following test, read each statement and check the box that best describes you. Even though the statements are focused specifically on you, ask the same questions of your department, division, management or executive team, and company.

The businessThink Humility Test

	Yes	Sometimes	Ego alert
1. When someone is giving me credit for a job well done, I make sure to include others who also deserve credit, and I thank them for the compliment.	❑	❑	❑
2. I stay focused on creating value for the company, without weighing exclusively what every project or assignment will do for me financially or politically.	❑	❑	❑
3. I would be surprised if others described me as brashly aggressive rather than quietly ambitious.	❑	❑	❑
4. If it weren't for the people who surround me, I wouldn't be what (or where) I am today.	❑	❑	❑
5. I don't perceive humility to be a weakness, but rather an asset of character.	❑	❑	❑
6. When other people are wrong (or make a mistake), and I am right, I am anxious to be inclusive of them moving forward, and I work to give them dignity.	❑	❑	❑

RULE 2

Create
Curiosity

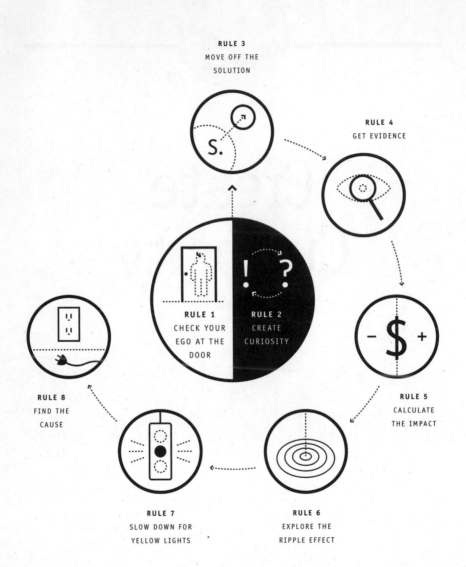

RULE 3
MOVE OFF THE
SOLUTION

RULE 4
GET EVIDENCE

S.

RULE 1
CHECK YOUR
EGO AT THE
DOOR

RULE 2
CREATE
CURIOSITY

RULE 8
FIND THE
CAUSE

− $ +

RULE 5
CALCULATE
THE IMPACT

RULE 7
SLOW DOWN FOR
YELLOW LIGHTS

RULE 6
EXPLORE THE
RIPPLE EFFECT

Curiosity is the driving force behind businessThinking. Humility clears the path to solutions, and curiosity provides the motivation to find them. All great performers, regardless of their field of expertise, seem to have it. Often their genius is credited to good DNA, but we believe the true essence of their greatness is a skill that can be refined. Every company starts with an idea, and every idea started with someone who was curious. Scott Cook, one of the founders of Intuit, got the idea for his Quicken software by watching his wife pay bills the old way. Everybody asks questions, but someone who is intensely curious gets more information than others even when asking the very same question.

> **The only real "factory asset" you have is your imagination, and curiosity drives imagination.**

Without an intense desire to dig deep into underlying issues, complex problems will rarely be solved—and neither will simple ones. Without curiosity, people walk past opportunities to make their companies better. Curiosity shows a willingness to look beyond past experience and consider the past, present, and future. When we talk about unleashing curiosity, we are not talking about letting loose like a wild, furious Tasmanian devil devouring everything in its path. Just asking a litany of questions is harassment, not curiosity.

If you blow up a balloon, and then let go of the stem of the balloon, it zigs and zags all over the place as the air escapes, then falls to the ground. If you add structure to the principle of thrust (like wings and a tail), this principle now can be used to power a great tool (an airplane) to take you to specific destinations with great speed and accuracy. Curiosity is what allows people to bring flexibility and improvement to things that are stale, rigid, and unchanging, and structure to chaos that serves nobody. Curiosity in businessThink is disciplined, and has a very specific intent—to create a solution that *exactly* meets the company's needs. Connect form or structure to your curiosity, and it will pay big-time dividends. The good news is that being investigative by nature isn't held in reserve for the playful or the creative types. It's not stashed away for the people in product development or owned by ad agencies. It's for everyone. Digging deep for the right answers is the spirit of exploration.

Creating curiosity will give you the tools to explore new options, open minds, and create an atmosphere or culture of asking "what if" questions that get to the heart of the matter. It will give you insights into your business you haven't considered before, become a vital source of more great ideas, and leverage the intellectual diversity and power of thinking in your company.

• CHAPTER FOUR •

The Deep Dive
for Curiosity

As part of our work we regularly conduct interviews and video-tape sessions in the course of studying the behavior of top performers from companies like EDS, CSC, Accenture, Microsoft, and others. While these individual performers have unique personalities and styles, nearly all of them share one common trait—curiosity. If we look beyond our own research, it's no surprise the same trait shows up in other successful people and companies. Great performers, whether in sports, entertainment, or business, seem to have no shortage of curiosity. Martha Stewart and Steve Jobs have it. There's no question that Frederick Taylor, Thomas Edison, and Albert Einstein all had it. We would also like to introduce you to someone you probably haven't heard of, Grace Murray Hopper. She had it, too.

Hopper's efforts changed the face of computer programming. Computer code used to be written only in numbers or binary code. This made writing code, or finding mistakes in what was written, very tedious and difficult. She started to wonder why the foundation had to be numbers, and suggested an unusual alternative. Though everyone thought she was crazy, and said it couldn't be done, she persisted. Eventually, she invented the COBOL programming language, which made it possible to convert those endless lines of numbers into English words. This was such an astonishing breakthrough that she was the first person to receive *Computer Science*'s "Man" of the Year Award.[1]

She was never *assigned* to do what she did, and it was not part of her job description—she just did it, much as Frederick Taylor tracked motion and movement. She used to have a clock in her office that ran counterclockwise to remind herself of the principle underlying her success. The impact of her curiosity was literally to change the world, especially the business world. Without her discovery, it's unlikely that Bill Gates would have had any beginning language to create Windows from, or that you would be able to surf the Web today.

Intense, Boundless Curiosity

> The soul of businessThink is curiosity, and *not* just run-of-the-mill, mild-mannered inquiry. We're talking intense, boundless inquiry.

We've found that the curious ask questions—penetrating questions that get to the heart of the matter—and not merely questions of facts and data gathering, but questions that dig into possibilities, outcomes, and options. Those who get curious often get it right—no matter what—and this leads to a tangible competitive advantage. Here's a case in point:

In 1999, ABC News aired a *Nightline* broadcast titled "The Deep Dive," about a company named IDEO, possibly the most influential and innovative product development firm in the world.[2] IDEO designs 90 new products every year, ranging from high-tech medical devices to toothbrush handles. Some of the company's designs include the first Apple computer mouse, Nike sunglasses, the mechanical whale in *Free Willy*, Scott ski goggles, and microwave ovens. ABC challenged IDEO to redesign the most basic of everyday items—a shopping cart—and bring it into the twenty-first century, in five days!

As the group members tackled ABC's challenge, they applied the same process to the shopping cart as they would to any other product. You might expect to see *only* a bunch of wacky, off-the-wall types that dive right into a brainstorming session. Not so. First, they enact intense curiosity *before* they get creative. It would have been easy to skip the fact-finding phase since every one of them was an "authority" on shopping carts, having personally pushed them around for years. After all, a shopping cart couldn't be that difficult to figure out, given the collective experience of the group. Besides, they had only five days for the redesign, so they needed to hurry. But they resisted the temptation to cut corners.

The team members interviewed shoppers, talked to store owners, asked store employees questions, took pictures of people shopping (with and without children), did research on shopping cart safety (20,000 hospitalizations a year), shopped themselves (with different awareness this time), and found out that carts whipped by wind in parking lots have been clocked at 35 miles per hour. In short, they went crazy asking questions! They were more like a bunch of anthropologists than designers. In order to understand as much as they possibly could outside their own knowledge, these designers got up from their desks, and went out on the street (aisles) where shopping actually happens. They went to *other* experts to gain critical insight from other varying perspectives, and gathered as much evidence as they could. As a rule, they routinely go to live with the unknown and explore what's unfamiliar to them. The spirit of Frederick Taylor is alive and well at IDEO.

What the group created in the end was nothing short of revolutionary. The new shopping cart had a built-in high-tech scanner that logged in prices of the items inserted into the cart, eliminating the need to stand in long checkout lines or wonder about prices. The cart's wheels turned 90 degrees so you could push the cart from side to side; no more lifting the back end up to change positions or get out of someone's way. The traditional big metal basket of the cart was replaced with smaller, mobile hand baskets that could easily be removed and put back onto the cart, so you could leave your cart and run quickly down the aisle to fill up the minibaskets.

With the innovative output that springs from this kind of curiosity, other firms are hard pressed to stay within reach of IDEO's success. IDEO could have simply redesigned the shopping cart and given it an ergonomic feel. They could have manufactured it out of different, lighter-weight materials. Perhaps the changes would have been good, but chances are they would have been missing a great deal of what was possible. As a creative design company, IDEO didn't just rely on "creativity" or "design," although both are crucial elements for brilliant output. What fueled their creative process were the answers to the questions they asked *before* they started innovating. If they hadn't learned as much as possible about what was outside their own knowledge and expertise, their creativity would likely have been limited to above-average output.

The question remains: How do they temporarily set aside their "creative genius," and their experiences with successful product innovations of the past, as they approach each new project? Tom Kelley tells us.

> *It's a funny paradox. Though we're pretty confident in our ability to observe people and draw insights out of them, we pride ourselves on starting every project humbly—and a little dumb. We don't want to peek at the answers before we know the questions.*
>
> —Tom Kelley, General Manager, IDEO[3]

IDEO is supposed to be curious, right? So should every other company on the planet! The very essence of businessThink is to enact that kind of curiosity about everything, with every person, in every company.

You should enter every project "humbly—and a little dumb." No peeking at the answers before asking questions. Find out what you don't know. Make room in your head for additional information that can improve on what you already know, and what you have experienced. Nothing is taken away if you temporarily let go of what you do know.

What You *Do* Know Could Hurt You

It might surprise you, but what you *currently* know often gets in the way of what you *need* to know, but don't. It serves as a filter that can limit curiosity, in you and others. The knowledge you gain from your experiences and learning leads to beliefs. When you think you know something, it's easy to get sucked into thinking that there is no longer a need to slow down and ask questions or consider other viewpoints. That's where the problems begin.

The passion and grip with which we hold onto beliefs blocks curiosity.

People even talk about beliefs in possessive ways: I don't *buy* that; you *hold* a belief or *cling* to your opinions or *defend* your position, or else you *lose* faith and *abandon* your convictions. The disease of conformity and indifference sets in when you coast on what you already know, and although it may take some time before the symptoms of intellectual apathy show up in results, they inevitably will.

For example, there was a furniture store that was having a problem with sales in electronics. After somewhere between 18 months and two years on the job, the top salespeople would unexpectedly slip into a tailspin, and their individual sales would nose-dive. In an attempt to spot the difference, researchers watched veterans and compared them to the rookies just learning the ropes. It turned out that six months was about the time it took for salespeople to learn all there was to know about the products they were selling. As a result, the veterans didn't ask clients as many questions as the rookies did. The more they came to know, the more they talked and tried to impress customers with how much they knew about the product. When a customer came in, they would simply blab on about the features and benefits of the product. *They stopped asking questions!*

In contrast, the rookies didn't know anything about the product itself, so they were anxious to keep the discussion focused on the customers and their needs. Because they had little to tell, they were forced to get better at asking questions. In the end, management attributed the sales problem primarily to too much product knowledge. They solved this problem by rotating salespeople every 18 months to a new department, such as appliances or computers, to keep the curiosity alive.

Every time you revert back to only what you already know, you prevent yourself from gaining a deeper understanding that would allow you to get it right for yourself, your company, and your clients. Stay open rather than allowing yourself to close down.

> Be a sponge for information and use it to refresh your experience and knowledge rather than allowing yourself to feel as if new information puts you at risk.

You can tell when others are unwilling to let go and explore, to stay open. For instance, maybe you have seen someone shake their head no while you were in the *middle* of sharing your idea (maybe you've done this to others, too). Early on in the explanation of your idea, they heard something that didn't match what they "knew," and it evoked an automatic reaction. They were already mentally closing you, your idea, and any exploration down, and their body language was letting you know to stop because your ideas weren't being heard. Judgment had set in. Often, new ideas are judged against what is accepted as possible, plausible, or reasonable.

Mental "head shaking" places limits on what's possible (in your head) versus what's *really* possible, between what you *think* is going on, and what really *is* going on. Blind or unyielding acceptance of what is known sacrifices the unknown, which may hold the key to something better. We're not talking about some ethereal, twilight-zone unknown, but the simple pursuit of getting to the heart of the matter to make sure your thinking is accurate and complete. If your thinking is not, don't expect a solution that is accurate or complete. The physical creation is rarely much better than the thinking or mental creation behind it.

Change Your Belief Wardrobe

Consider for a moment how people buy clothes. When your clothes wear out, or go out of style, it usually happens a few pieces at a time. If you update your wardrobe as things wear out, it's easy to stay current. Most people look for things that match what they already have in their wardrobe, can be used interchangeably, and fit personal style. Beliefs are like an intellectual wardrobe: People continually try to match their beliefs and "buy" things that fit their mental ensemble and suit their intellectual style. In contrast, when their ideas "wear out," or "don't fit" anymore, rather than replace them with something more functional, they try harder to force the fit. There are corporate wardrobes as well, and they, too, stay coordinated, in step, and within the boundaries of the corporate mental closet.

> *The longer we've lived and breathed the air of a particular corporate culture, and developed behaviors and beliefs in response to that culture, the more likely we are to treat beliefs (or history) as fact, and honor every company "wardrobe item" as holy tradition.*

In a business world where the rules change (a lot), and the landscape can look different every day (or at least quarterly), be prepared to unleash your curiosity. In a changing, evolving world, mental models need to be refreshed constantly.

For example, we participated in a meeting recently, trying to help people decide on brand design as part of a new product launch. When the ideas were presented, there were strong reactions around the room, favorable and unfavorable. Someone in the meeting instantly compared the ideas to her own experience, and formed a bias about what *would* work and what *wouldn't*. When she shared her opinion about the value of different options, she began her statement with, "I've been doing [this] since 1992, and these designs will work, these won't, and that's just the way it works because. . . ." She instantly dismissed everything that was outside her experience. The assumption she was operating on, and expected everyone else to adopt, was that anything since 1992 has followed, and must follow, the same exact rules in order to succeed.

> Throughout the history of scientific thought most laymen have been so anxious for certainty and have had such low tolerance for ambiguity and change that they have been eager to say that a theory is a fact.
>
> **—STEPHEN R. COVEY**

We're not suggesting she should throw out her beliefs with reckless abandon, and dismiss everything she has learned since 1992. The lessons from a decade of learning are important ones, but only as they are kept fresh by a willingness to add to experience, to have things change for the better. Curiosity is about keeping your beliefs fresh and in tune with what's going on. This is where genuine confidence will give you the courage to be curious without worrying about not straying too far from the past. Rather than holding to what worked 10, 5, even 3 years ago, stay open to what might work right now, or even to what might be able to work better that's different. The more you fight to validate your experience, the more you risk losing insight that can keep your experience current in a business landscape that changes frequently.

> **In times of change, learners inherit the earth, while the learned find themselves beautifully equipped to deal with a world that no longer exists.**
>
> **–ERIC HOFFER, *THE ORDEAL OF CHANGE*[4]**

What's in Your Company's Belief Closet?

If you are not careful, especially in groups, the only thoughts that wind up being mixed and matched are those that are already in the closet. "No need to ask questions here" becomes the corporate mind-set. A company can end up with the collective mental equivalent of orange polyester pants and a denim leisure jacket (no offense, if that's your style). Intellectual apathy breeds clones: Every mouth eventually says the same thing, and every brain is washed to share the same ideas.

> *Beliefs are like possessions. We acquire and attain material possessions because of the functions they serve and the value they offer. To some extent the same can be said of our beliefs. We may be particularly inclined to acquire and retain beliefs that make us feel good.*
> —Thomas Gilovich, *How We Know What Isn't So*[5]

Let's return briefly to the story of IDEO. The company values diversity—and not just differences in ethnic origin, religion, or political leaning. They deliberately hire people of incredible intellectual diversity—people who aren't conformists in their thinking and who have diverse, varied backgrounds. The project team was comprised of a linguist, a psychologist, a marketing expert, a biology student, an engineer, and a Harvard MBA. Breakthrough solutions come from curiosity, and curiosity thrives on *intellectual* diversity.

> The enlightened trial and error that comes from intellectual diversity and intense, insatiable curiosity succeeds over the planning of the lone genius.

Titles, Egos, and History Be Damned!

Hierarchy (titles and positions) can be an enemy of curiosity, even if you're fortunate enough to have intellectual diversity. Titles and positions lead you to believe you know more than you actually do (as if total insight came with the position). Ask yourself these questions:

- *If you're in a meeting, and the boss is there, how curious are people allowed to be?* If the boss speaks *first,* everyone else will follow that line of thinking. If the boss speaks *last,* everyone will stretch to find some way to bend their ideas to fit the last thing shared by the boss. It's not unusual for companies to develop corporate knowledge and experience that unwittingly extinguish curiosity. If you're going to build a curious corporation, you have to have a level playing field.

- *If you happen to be the boss, how are you going to get people to open up?* The answer is to make sure no rewards are given for blind obedience to what you say. If someone succeeds, and you weren't in on it, make them a hero. Hold them up as an example. People who succeed in spite of you, and then are not invited to "play" more often, end up leaving, and others quickly get the message to fall in line or leave. When hierarchy is tyrannical, the curious and courageous buck the system (if you're lucky, and they haven't left for the competition) with questions that are considered by others to be taboo, that risk personal, political safety or security, and that fly in the face of politics as usual. These people virtually ignore position and standing because the real answers aren't found *because* of someone's title or position.

They are unabashedly in pursuit of what's best, what works, and the best way to do it. Titles, egos, and history be damned!

Jack Welch tells the story of one of General Electric's hierarchy-breaking workout sessions:

> I'll never forget attending one of the workout sessions in 1990 in our appliance business. A union production worker was in the middle of a presentation on how to improve the manufacturing of refrigerator doors. He was describing the process that occurred on the second floor of the assembly line. Suddenly, the chief steward of the plant jumped up to interrupt him. "That's BS. You don't know what the hell you're talking about. You've never been up there." He grabbed a Magic Marker and began scribbling on the easel in front of the room. Before you knew it, he had taken over the presentation and had the answer. The solution was accepted immediately.[6]

Not a big surprise that one of the greatest legacies Welch left was that people began to forget their roles and titles, and focused on the business. The chief steward probably could have handled his suggestion with a bit more tact, but congratulations to the other guy for checking his ego and not disrupting a better idea. One of the appliance business workers said later, "For 25 years you've paid for my hands when you could have had my brain as well—for nothing."

An abandonment of hierarchy is not always the standard operating procedure for noncurious companies. For example, we consulted with a vice president of research and development on a product idea that required expertise the company lacked. They were short on the technical competence needed to deliver on the strategy, yet people wouldn't question the existing strategy because it would represent a challenge to the competence and wisdom of the executive team. The pressure to appear all-knowing and all-wise can make for some strange (and bad) decisions. The curious aren't afraid of mistakes, nor are they afraid to speak boldly, nobly, and independently—and not just for the sake of being heard, but for the sake of a better outcome. In the end, the product took five months to develop, did little more than break even financially, and consumed months of time and focus from dozens of people, not to mention the opportunity costs of not working on projects with higher return on investment (ROI). No company exists to break even.

> *The [person] who focuses on efforts and who stresses [his or her] downward authority is a subordinate no matter how exalted [his or her] title and rank. But the [person] who focuses on contribution and takes responsibility for results, no matter how junior, is in the most literal sense of the phrase, "top management."*
> —Peter Drucker, *The Effective Executive*[7]

Extinguished Curiosity

Often, when my (Steve's) own children aren't curious, it's because I've created too much dependence on me for thinking, so much so that they blindly go through the motions without thinking for themselves. Just the other day my three sons came into the office where I was working and asked, "Dad, we're bored [said with more whining than writing can possibly express]. What should we do?" I couldn't believe they were interrupting me to ask what they should do! And then it occurred to me in a miniepiphany that I usually solve their boredom problem. I have traditionally, unknowingly, encouraged that mind-set by telling them what they should do.

This time I didn't answer, and they eventually solved the boredom problem on their own. Sometimes boredom is the instigator of curiosity in kids. As a dad, when I don't create any space for the light of exploration and thinking, I find I'm not raising problem solvers or decision makers, but dependent copycats. As soon as boredom sets in, I become the broker for ideas.

What kind of company culture are you creating or raising? A team of inquisitive thinkers or copycats? Dependent doers or interdependent thinkers? What responsibility are you taking away from people who need to stay curious?

What If You've Lost the Curiosity Groove?

So what if you've lost curiosity—how do you get your groove back? The first step may be to break out of your routine. Someone who isn't curious isn't likely to change the minute-to-minute routine of their day. Try something different.

Drive a different way to work, eat a different breakfast, wake up at a different time, enter through a different door, take on a project you wouldn't usually accept. Change the channel, listen to a different radio station—*anything* to notice new things, and then make notes. What was different? What would you change if you could? A lot of people don't get into the action because they are surrounded by routine, by sameness. Variety is a spark for curiosity.

> *Curiosity must be enacted. It must be a living, breathing force inside of your head and heart, and inside your company. Curiosity must have soul.*

The Soul of Curiosity

Building collective, corporate curiosity will require both the technique and the soul. I (Dave) spent nine years taking private piano lessons. I learned the scales, and developed the technical skill needed to play the music, yet I would listen to virtuosos play and I knew that my music didn't sound like theirs. I played all the *same notes* they were playing, but when they played, the music came *alive!* My music was the sound of notes coming from the piano, and theirs was the sound of music coming from the soul. So, what does this have to do with curiosity?

Until I became curious enough to find out what would make the difference in my music, my music stayed the same. I incessantly asked questions of my teacher and others. They described the difference between playing an instrument and becoming one with the instrument. They described how important it was to tie a story to the music to involve your feelings. I tried different things. I changed my approach. Then it happened. I became lost in the instrument, the music, and the story. Once I learned how to get the feeling inside me, and let it come out through my music, it profoundly changed the power of my music and the way I play. Now people come to me after a performance and tell me they *feel* my music.

In some ways, the soul of business is curiosity. It has deep feeling, and people feel a tangible difference when you have it. You can ask questions with *technical* curiosity, but it won't produce the same result as when you *feel* curious.

The Chief Curiosity Officer

If you want to inject that soul into your company, we propose one staffing change in your company: Every company should have an informal (or formal) *chief curiosity officer* (CCO), whose primary role is to inject curiosity into the corporate bloodstream. Not just a devil's advocate, but one who takes an opposite point of view with the intent of breaking people out of intellectual ruts and old paradigms. Someone once said, "A rut is a grave with both ends kicked out." Sadly, some people think the rut is a groove, and they haven't lost their groove. Maybe you can start the trend to break people, and your company, out of their grooves.

So what does a CCO do? The answer is *businessThink!* The chief curiosity officer is the person who could walk into any meeting, in any department, with anyone, on any topic, and create corporate curiosity. How? That's what businessThink is designed to do. Imagine the CCO moving around the halls and in and out of meetings.

The CCO might pop into one meeting and apply:

Rule 3: Move Off the Solution. No matter the topic, move off the solution to the underlying issues that need to be addressed. For example, imagine the team is engaged in a discussion about the features and benefit of a solution, and the CCO asks questions to make sure the business issues are robust and relevant to the matter at hand: Is the list complete? Could we be missing something?

Another meeting is happening somewhere in marketing, and the CCO dives into the discussion to apply:

Rule 4: Get Evidence. What proves we have a problem? What? How? When? Where? Who? Everybody starts to search, dig, and find the evidence. If we do that, then what happens? If we have this, what would that allow us to do?

From there the CCO shows up as human resources is closing a discussion on a new recruitment strategy, and makes the move to apply:

Rule 5: Calculate the Impact. What is the impact, financially or strategically, on the company? What's the value of the difference between the recruiting strategy we have now, and what we want? How will we know we're successful? What is it now? What would we like it to be?

Rule 6: Explore the Ripple Effect.   Who or what else is affected by the problem or opportunity? If we move on these ideas, how will that affect others?

Rule 7: Slow Down for Yellow Lights.   If this is such a big deal, what has stopped us in the past? What is likely to stop us if we do this in the future?

Rule 8: Find the Cause.   Why is this happening? Are these symptoms or causes?

The rules of businessThink are *designed for curiosity.* The chief curiosity officer walks around the company with a curiosity conscience. Imagine you have a person (e.g., an angel, a devil, Jiminy Cricket—choose an icon or persona for your conscience) on your shoulder who's always whispering in your ear: "What if . . . ?" "This is really interesting. What are the reasons for . . . ?" "It seems like we have thought of just about everything. Did we think about . . . ?" "What are all the other options . . . ?"

> **Make the move from thinking with a big exclamation point to a perpetual question mark!**

As you take on the role of CCO for your company, your department, or simply yourself, remember that the rules are the "scales" of businessThink, but without the soul of *curiosity,* you will have only had the technique, and technique will take you only so far. The soul of curiosity breathes life into *what we do* to find solutions and make decisions. Without soul, the technique may be there, but the most powerful insight, the 10 percent that could make the difference, remains elusive. You've heard the old saying, "Familiarity breeds contempt." *Good!* Maybe it should! If people were a little more contemptuous of familiar thinking, they could shake themselves out of some pretty tough problems and into some much-needed solving. The checklist in the following section, and those for the businessThink rules that follow, will serve to provide you with some self-awareness of your performance as a chief curiosity officer, whether the title is officially designated or unofficially adopted. These lists may give you a glimpse of what's inside the arteries of your company.

Even if you have years of experience and well-developed expertise, stay intensely, insanely curious. As a young mother with absolutely no business experience, Anita Roddick founded the Body Shop in 1976. Twenty-five years later, her company is a sensation, with over 1,700 stores around the world and 84 million customers. Roddick may be the ultimate personification of a curious businesswoman who reinvented business.

In her book, *Business as Unusual,* Roddick outlines the qualities you need to be a natural, curious entrepreneur. As the founder of the Body Shop, she attributes a large part of her success to curiosity:

> I don't believe you have to go to college and study at the feet of some nutty professor of entrepreneurship. I think you have to ask questions of everyone, and never stop asking questions, and knock on doors to seek as many different opinions as exist. It's not the theories that interest me and excite me—it's the doing.
>
> When I was in a market in India, I saw all these stainless steel cans for carrying water. I looked at that volume of shapes all in the same material and thought what wonderful packaging they would make. San Francisco is famous for its sour dough bread. When I was there I began wondering what it would be like if you made a raw sour dough mixture and washed your body with it. I am always thinking of things that might go on the hair and body, looking at different textures, different ideas.[8]

She may own the Body Shop, but what started the wildly successful company was her own, personal curiosity shop. Not only is there a return on investment for the Body Shop, there is also a big-time return on curiosity.

Balance your own limited views with the perspective of others. *Curiosity,* like *business,* is a verb, not a noun. You won't be curious sitting at your desk. You need to leave, change environments, investigate, dig, and search. Curiosity says, "I don't know, and I am dying to find out." In other words, **Ask! Wonder! Question! Ponder! Speculate! Hypothesize! Think! Think! Think!** If Roger Banister had not asked the curious question, "Why has no one been able to break the four-minute mile?" he also wouldn't have asked, "What do I have to do to break the barrier?" Intense curiosity is vital to high performance. If you don't have boundless curiosity, you will be far less successful in businessThinking, or anything else for that matter. Curiosity says, "*Wake up!*" It's simply that important. And it's simply not that common. You need that edge, and it's an edge only curiosity can deliver.

The businessThink Mirror

In the following test, read each statement and check the box that best describes you. Even though the statements are focused specifically on you, ask the same questions of your department, division, management or executive team, and company.

The businessThink Curiosity Test

	CCO*	Sometimes	Comfortably numb
1. I would say I enter most projects a little "humble and dumb." I'm willing to set aside what I know to learn something new.	❏	❏	❏
2. I actively seek out perspectives, viewpoints, and thoughts that are different from my own.	❏	❏	❏
3. My security isn't wrapped around what I know, and new ideas don't make me feel at risk.	❏	❏	❏
4. I would say my company embraces intellectual diversity. It's okay to disagree.	❏	❏	❏
5. When ideas are seen as unusual or nontraditional, people embrace exploring them rather than closing the discussion down.	❏	❏	❏
6. I am able to stay curious without getting off task or being inquisitive just for the sake of difference.	❏	❏	❏
7. People are rewarded in my company for being curious rather than just falling in line.	❏	❏	❏
8. Rather than simply going through the motions when I ask questions, I *feel* curious about the whole discovery process.	❏	❏	❏

*Chief curiosity officer

Note: If you would like to complete a more comprehensive and complimentary profile to score your businessThink effectiveness and measure it against others in our database who have taken the businessThink profile, please visit **www.businessthink.biz/profile**.

Move Off
the Solution

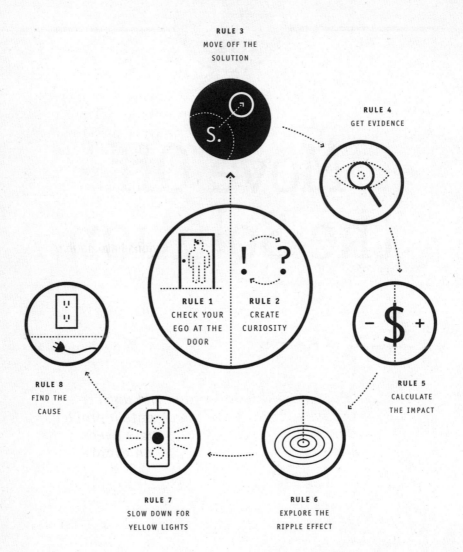

RULE 3
MOVE OFF THE
SOLUTION

RULE 4
GET EVIDENCE

RULE 1
CHECK YOUR
EGO AT THE
DOOR

RULE 2
CREATE
CURIOSITY

RULE 8
FIND THE
CAUSE

RULE 5
CALCULATE
THE IMPACT

RULE 7
SLOW DOWN FOR
YELLOW LIGHTS

RULE 6
EXPLORE THE
RIPPLE EFFECT

The definitive outcome of businessThinking is a rock-solid, near-perfect solution. That's the ultimate businessThink objective. However, *solution* has become an overhyped, mind-numbing buzzword. The word *solution* is being preached from every business pulpit, and we've lost touch with what the word really means. Everyone has a solution, and lays claim to the phrase *solution provider*. The question is, do solutions mean *results*?

> Predetermined, premeditated, premature solutions have no *inherent* value. Zero!

According to our best calculations, it doesn't matter what you multiply zero by—it still comes up zero.

Even when *decisive* people create "solutions" at lightning speed, they still have no value.

> *A solution is worthless unless and until it creates business value—until it prevents a problem or invents a new result the business needs. Otherwise, a solution is merely an event.*

It might be a cool, entertaining, funded event—but it's still only an event, and events amount to nothing but costs. Events, cleverly disguised as real solutions, are the false gods people worship at the altar of business.

Moving Off the Solution will give you the tools to quickly get to the underlying business issues that need to be addressed through the solution. It will bring clarity and definition to the issues by focusing attention and dialogue on the vital few.

CHAPTER FIVE

Welcome to the Main Event

Imagine for a moment that you are four years old, and someone makes the following deal with you: They will give you a big, yummy marshmallow right now, no strings attached. Just for being you. It's all yours. If you can wait a few minutes though, and not eat the marshmallow while they run a quick errand, they'll give you two marshmallows when they get back (which is great return on investment [ROI] for you as a four-year-old!). It's enough to try the mettle of any preschooler.

This very proposal was made in real research conducted by Walter Minshel at Stanford University in the late 1960s. Four- and five-year-old preschoolers were brought into a room with a small table and chair and asked to wait 15 to 20 minutes (an eternity to a child being tempted by a treat) while the researcher ran "an errand." Imagine you were watching what was going on from behind a two-way mirror. Here is what you would have seen.

For some of the kids, there was no space between stimulus and response—it was as if there were a string attached from the door to the marshmallow, and from the marshmallow to their mouths. The moment the researcher left the room and closed the door—*Gulp!* The marshmallow quickly disappeared into their mouths.

For other children, you could see the struggle! They *wanted* to eat it now—but they also wanted two marshmallows. A few of the children pretended it wasn't there and wandered around the room. Some sang, while others talked to themselves. And from across the room, the marshmallow seemed to beckon, "Eat meee!"

Some kids, giving in to the overwhelming need to put the marshmallow out of its misery, considered eating it. And picking it up, they *licked* it! This was okay, because technically they had not *eaten* the marshmallow. Other children sat in front of the marshmallow with their faces buried in their hands, or their hands covering their eyes. Occasionally you would see them peek between their fingers to see if the marshmallow had moved, and then quickly cover their eyes back up. The ultimate in resistance was when kids actually climbed under the table and fell asleep.

After observing their initial reactions, researchers followed these children over the next 20 years or so. Here's what they found: Years later, as young men and women, those who resisted their impulses and waited for the two-marshmallow ROI, showed better skills under stress, embraced challenges, and pursued goals rather than giving up in the face of difficulties. They were also more confident, trustworthy, dependable, and willing to take initiative than those who ate the marshmallow instantly. They also scored an average of 200 points higher (out of a possible 1,600) on the Scholastic Aptitude Test (SAT) college entrance exam. Amazing stuff. The researchers also concluded that children at that young age were incapable of delaying gratification, but they had somehow learned strategies for shifting their focus or attention to something else for the better ROI.[1]

Addicted to Events

Events are the business version of the marshmallow. Businesspeople are the kids in the room, impulsively waiting to devour the marshmallow. The *real* solution, with the highest ROI, is the whole bag of marshmallows, but they can't resist. They don't think first—they grab what's in front of them and shove it in their mouths. The thunderous wake-up call to all of us as businesspeople is "Don't eat the marshmallow!" The one marshmallow in front of you could be nothing more than an event—a *could,* not a solution. Wait for the real thing. Intellectually, it's not too hard to grasp this concept. Psychologically and emotionally, it's hard to accept.

There is perhaps no psychological skill more fundamental than resisting impulse.

—DANIEL GOLEMAN, *EMOTIONAL INTELLIGENCE*[2]

Events are sexy. Sometimes people would like to think there is a magic bullet; that you can throw some money at a situation and everything will be okay. Talking about the event gives us mental adrenaline, and so there is a mutual conspiracy among everyone to talk about a solution before we really understand the underlying issues, evidence, and financial impact of what would create the solution we need.

The Main Event

Here is an example that could easily be the poster child for *events.* Not long ago, I (Dave) was part of a cross-functional team that had the responsibility of implementing an enterprise resource planning system. This represented a complete replacement of the company's technology infrastructure. This was not a small undertaking; we were replacing everything, from our call-center order-entry system to manufacturing to distribution and inventory planning. We talked with very experienced outsiders who dangled enticing and proven methodologies as *events* for success. We hired two companies to help us scope it and identify a budget. The board of directors approved the initial budget of $27 million, fully loaded, and the team started down the long, winding road with the *hope* of a big return.

Hope is not a method. Nor is it a strategy.

Once a decision is made on a solution to a particular problem, meetings seem to multiply like rabbits. We were no different, and we were world-class at it. If meeting were an Olympic sport, we were the gold medalists. We met on strategy, direction, team composition, timelines, budgets, buy-in, all phases of implementation, and end-user requirements, ad nauseum. We even met on the meetings we were going to have.

Along a stretch of freeway where we live there is a billboard for a technical college that says:

Get in. Get out. Make $$$.

That's what this initiative, and our meetings, should have been about. The long story short is that we ultimately ended up with a fully loaded price tag of $54 million. Good return for the out-siders, and all the *company* got out of it was a good set of financial reporting software. That's it. Oh, and some human resource stuff. If we had known exactly what we were *actually* going to get *before* we started, we could have done it for around $2 million. And that $2 million could have delivered a rock-solid return rather than mor-phing into a $54 million cost. We *thought* we knew what we wanted to *prevent* and *invent,* and it ended up as a multi-million-dollar, multiyear *event.* If we'd had a billboard for *this* project it would have read, "Get in. *Stay* in. *Spend* $$$." We were so desper-ate for a solution that we were willing to accept an event where the investment *I* devoured the return *R*.

No More Events

David House, a former Intel executive who left to become the CEO of Bay Networks, a troubled manufacturer of high-tech equipment that was competing against giants such as Cisco and 3Com, would be on the right side of the solution spectrum. When House took over Bay Networks, rather than doing the typical turnaround stuff like announcing layoffs, liquidating divisions, revi-sioning, remissioning, retooling, centralizing, and decentralizing, he *taught courses.* He *personally* taught courses on what he believed to be fundamental and basic to business: thinking like businesspeople, making decisions, disagreeing openly, engaging in straight talk, managing for results, and focusing on what's important. Eventually, everyone in the company was "House-trained."

House applied his version of businessThinking to the company's most serious problems, and taught people new ways of working. With well-trained businesspeople, solutions took over events.

Solutions were funded, events got cancelled, and resources were reallocated to real, priority issues. Bay Networks began to develop a shared "mental operating system" that led to a culture of business-ready, decision-savvy people. Bay Networks recovered from its $285-million loss in fiscal 1997, posting $89 million in profits in the first six months of fiscal 1998. The following June, Nortel agreed to buy Bay Networks in a deal valued at $9 billion.[3]

In telling this story we don't intend for you to believe that once you businessThink, the sun, moon, and stars will all somehow magically align themselves. Nortel is currently tanking. House is no longer at the helm. If you had bought $1,000 worth of Nortel stock one year ago as of this writing, it would now be worth $49. If you had bought $1,000 worth of Budweiser (the beer, not the stock) one year ago, drank all the beer, and traded in the cans for the nickel deposit, you would have $79. Stuff happens, conditions change, and businessThinking always needs to be responsive to evolve with the feedback each decision elicits. Since a solution's *physical* creation rarely unfolds as it was envisioned in the *mental* creation, perfectly intended consequences are rare.

Just Because You Can Doesn't Mean You Should!

What hurts businesses, often fatally, is focusing on the things they *could* be doing, and not enough on the things they *should* be doing. There is a poignant scene in the movie *Jurassic Park* in which Jeff Goldblum, who plays a mathematician and theorist named Dr. Malcolm, is invited to evaluate Jurassic Park scientifically. As he and other colleagues are having dinner with the inventor and creator of the park, John Hammond, Hammond is explaining the great discoveries of science that have never been made before. At this point in the conversation Malcolm interrupts and says, "I'll tell you the problem with the scientific power that you're using here; it didn't require any discipline to attain it. . . . You stood on the shoulders of geniuses to accomplish something as fast as you could and before you even knew what you had you patented it and packaged it and slapped it on a lunchbox. . . . Your scientists were so preoccupied with whether or not they could, that they didn't stop to think if they should."

When businessThink is working, it answers the Jurassic Park question: Of all the things you *could* do as a business, what are the vital few you *should* do? Are you so preoccupied with *coulds* that you don't stop to think whether you *should?* Just because you *can* doesn't mean you *should.* The *coulds* are okay when thinking through the issues, but when they are not killed and live to drain corporate resources, *coulds* are dangerous distractions. If you had all the time, people and money in the world, you could enthusiastically spend it, and wait to see what worked and what failed. That's not how business works. With *unlimited* choices and *limited* resources, *coulds* have killed a lot of businesses. Making the move from all of the *coulds* to the relevant *shoulds* means the decisions you make will lead to solutions (not events) that produce big-time return or impact for the time, people, and money invested. This is where the business reality of ROI enters the picture.

> **Business is not solely a cause. Causes, and even great ideas, can be compelling, inspiring, and still go out of business quickly—just ask the start-ups. It's not just about a mission. In business, there is no mission without money.**

This doesn't mean you should dismiss your mission, ideas, talent, creativity, intellectual freedom, vision, or anything else. It does mean that unless those things result in ROI—unless they deliver impact—they're dead. We're not saying that's good or bad. It just *is.* If ROI is in fact embraced, and solutions are still dead on arrival, then it's the ideas and decisions you should be gravely concerned about.

> *Profit is like oxygen, food, water, and blood for the body; they are not the point of life, but without them, there is no life.*
> —Jim Collins and Jerry Porras, *Built to Last*[4]

The missing piece in many decisions is an accurate, complete picture of the R (return) part of the ROI equation. ROI is the *whole* formula—it's not only the investment, nor is it simply about the return. Think about the last key decision you made or solution you saw ignited. How clear was the R to you and others? How clear was the return or impact to clients or the market? In far too many cases it's not easy to find, and many don't know how to get it. Or they have hastily and prematurely set their sights on the *I* (investment) part of the equation, often because they don't *really* believe in the return. The *I* turns into a *C* (cost), and costs without any return are *always* too high.

There is another ROI-like formula regularly used in business: *S − C = P*. *Sales* minus *costs* equals *profit*. The reason you want a solution in the first place is because you have a belief that the solution will either increase sales, decrease costs, or better leverage capital, any or all of which will have a net effect of increasing profits. Frequently, the event selected and implemented actually *gets in the way* of sales or *drives up* costs (or both), which has the net effect of *shrinking* profits. The thinking behind every decision you make, every solution you create, affects the company. Measured or not, noticed or not, it will have an impact.

And in your pursuit of ROI and the *S* and *P* of *S − C = P*, you're bombarded by events that have the ring of a solution from every direction, department, vendor, company, and person you know. (You also do your fair share of bombarding others.) When you're feeling the immense pressure to solve, you often turn your attention to the features and benefits of the *coulds,* and you are deceived into believing that you are, in fact, solving. Features are just that: features—things. And benefits are only benefits if they're lined up with the real and relevant needs you're trying to address. Discussing features and benefits before you have identified the problem or clearly defined the opportunity is not real thinking; it's hallucinating. You're not the only one deliriously happy to dream; vendors will wax rhapsodic about the endless features and benefits of their "solutions." How many companies do you think have created the following *events* (to name only a few), thinking they were bona fide solutions, when in fact they were the *wrong* thing to do?

- Pursue customer segmentation.
- Adopt a lower pricing strategy.
- Merge or acquire a new business.
- Make the whole business an e-business.
- Initiate and structure an IPO.
- Restructure, reorganize, reengineer, rewhatever.

- Expand product lines.
- Form strategic alliances.
- Develop competency modeling.

All these are viable solutions if the problem or opportunity actually *matches* the solution. Otherwise, they're only events. You can probably quickly identify a number of lethal events you and others have administered to your company, Kervorkian style.

When events are mistaken for solutions, here are some of the downsides:

- Scarce, limited resources are siphoned from solutions to events.
- Everything becomes a priority, and almost nothing gets enough attention or focus to really succeed.
- Chronic problems aren't solved, and the pain of the symptoms becomes embedded in the daily culture that everyone, slowly, just lives with.
- Costs are driven up.
- New, compounded problems arise from the wrong solution.
- Time and attention are diverted to competing *coulds.*
- Activity is mistaken for productivity and progress.
- The crucial underlying business issues remain uncovered.

But if the addiction to fake solutions and events is so paralyzing, and often suicidal, how do you break the habit?

• CHAPTER SIX •

No More Guessing

When people offer a "solution," it's usually couched in words that are meaningful to them. When someone uses words that fit smoothly into a sentence, it's easy to make the mistake of assuming that they use the same meaning for the words as you do—and that's dangerous. We all guess that because we understand what something means to us, it must mean the same thing to everyone else. We assume we know what they mean, we assume they know what they mean, they assume we know what they mean, they assume we know what we mean, and no one has a clue—especially when it comes to company or technical jargon, buzzwords, and acronyms.

> The more an organization knows about a term or concept relevant to its business, the less likely it is to agree on a common term or meaning for it.
>
> **—THOMAS DAVENPORT, *INFORMATION ECOLOGY*[1]**

We've had 30-minute conversations with executives in which terms and phrases like "better alignment with our vision" and "we see the confluence of outside factors in our business" were flying around, and we were unclear what they meant. We had to ask, "What do you mean when you say _____?" five or six times. The fact that *they* had to think about it before answering let us know it was a good question to ask. We wanted to make sure that we understood what those terms meant to them. Merely asking the question helped them to stop and rethink about something they thought of as familiar and common to everyone.

Abstraction Poker

Often, people offer their ideas and talk about solutions in terms linguists call *complex equivalents* or *high-level abstractions*. These are words or phrases that encode many experiences and beliefs into one small package. Like an iceberg, the word floats above the surface, and the multiple meanings and interpretations lurk deep below (Figure 6.1). Rather than diving for the meaning, people often exchange mutual understanding for quick, easy memory access and explore only their own definitions, their own icebergs.

Have you ever heard someone say something, and you both then pretended to know what it meant and continued to have a conversation about it? We've all done this. William Isaacs, an expert on dialogue, calls these exchanges *abstraction wars.* A lot of conversa-

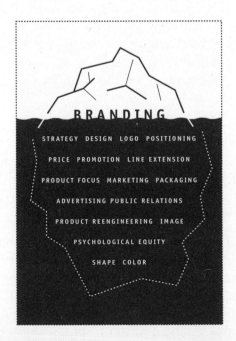

Figure 6.1   The tip of the abstraction iceberg.

tions consist of one person or department flinging an abstract word or description at you, and then you act as if what they said is clear and unmistakable, and throw one back. It's like you're playing conversational poker: "I'll see your abstraction, and raise you one!"[2]

> *The greatest enemy of communication*
> *is the illusion of it.*
>
> —Pierre Martineau

The illusion of communication is abundant. For instance, you have more than likely experienced meetings where everyone nods their head, indicating that they understand and agree with the message. But later, as you and a colleague compare notes from the meeting, it often becomes apparent that you each have walked away with a *different* understanding. All the head nodding gives the illusion that everyone has interpreted the message in the same way and is on the same page. However, there is no mutual understanding.

> **Without a shared understanding or definition, you don't get the results you want because your definition of success is not shared.**

Your concept of success may not be inclusive of other functions and interpretations, but exclusive. Which by definition means that the standard of success either is exclusively yours, or will constantly be shifting and changing. Everyone will have their private, functional interpretation of what *should* be included in the definition of success, and you will get the unfortunate, predictable results.

What Do You Mean?

When communicating, listen carefully to the key words or phrases people use, and then ask what those words mean *to them*. It is astounding how often they will come back with something very useful and valuable, but different from what you expected. Slow down and listen. Don't blow past the words and guess.

For example, if you were in the information technology department and a division manager came to you and asked if you could help them with knowledge management, wouldn't you be tempted to prove how smart you were (ego) or launch into your technical expertise about what you *could* do for them? Rather than giving in to the temptation, don't guess about what the person means by *knowledge management*.

Colleague: Our division needs to leverage all our data with a powerful, robust knowledge-management system. Do you guys do that?

Old School: Absolutely. The infrastructure we have been putting into place is as robust as anything you'd ever want or need.

businessThink: We do. And interestingly enough, every department we help usually has a different sense of what it means. Do you mind if I ask—when you say "knowledge management," what all are you including in your definition?

Or, consider another example:

Colleague: I think we need to put together a team for finding new ways of enhancing client value by increasing our sources of market differentiation.

Old School: Yeah, definitely! In fact, that could help us leverage our competitive advantage, and drive it even further through line extending some of our brands.

businessThink: When you say "enhancing client value," what does that mean in the context of what you're thinking we need to accomplish? What, in your mind, specifically needs to be differentiated?

Now you're not guessing about the meaning, and neither are they. They get a chance to explain themselves and think about what they're trying to achieve as a business division, and you get the opportunity to learn more. Instead of mutual mystification, you get mutual understanding. Rather than mutually guessing, mutually explore beliefs and assumptions. Of course, that's not easy. The more you simply and consistently guess, the more you're assuming while also validating their own (and your own) assumptions—and all assumptions on both sides may be wrong.

The Danger of Assumptions

Assumptions are another brand of guessing. They are particularly insidious because they often happen unconsciously; you don't even realize you're guessing. Examine the possible assumptions of the very word *solution* in the phrase, "We need a *solution* to the problem." What could the assumptions be?

- The problem is *real;* it *exists;* it hasn't gone away or wasn't an illusion in the first place.
- There is *only one* problem. Several different problems aren't intertwined.
- It is *possible* to solve the problem.
- The problem has *only one* solution.
- Having this problem is bad; having a solution would be good.
- People *care* about finding a solution to the problem.
- We can measure the extent of the problem.
- Different people perceive the problem in the same way.
- It is possible to determine if the solution is valid.
- The solution would solve the *entire* problem.
- The cost of the solution is *less than* the cost of the problem.
- The solution wouldn't cause *more* problems or a *worse* problem.
- The solution will be valid over time.

This is only a sample of the assumptions you can make. Let's take a look at a big corporate assumption. From our perspective, Pets.com appears to have made some pretty big assumptions about their business and their market. First of all, there was the infamous sock puppet. It was a clever idea, funny—but who was that little sock talking to? A marketing consultant friend of ours said, "Pet owners see their pets as members of the family, not toys or objects. Pets.com was treating *pets* as the individual buyers, not the owners." What was the big assumption? That pets spend money. Everybody knows pets don't spend money; their owners do. Pets don't shop, and they don't use a mouse, have credit cards, or go online when they want something.

Another big assumption in the "just because you can means you should" category was that people would be interested in buying pet supplies online. Really? Were people really interested in getting their dog food and cat litter online? Maybe. Isn't that stuff available at the local grocery store where they're already going shopping anyway? When people don't challenge assumptions, not only are the assumptions often wrong, but the underlying business or market issues are not explored deeply enough to test the assumptions and self-correct the ideas or strategies to make them valid and workable.

Not only were their assumptions off track, the business mechanics weren't in place. Pets.com spent $21 million a quarter just to get people to their site, then they sold their product below cost and shipped it free. That only works when you're a kid at a lemonade stand and your mom and dad are the venture capitalists who are willing to take the losses and give you all the profits.

What were they thinking? They forgot that building a great brand with memorable and funny commercials couldn't change the fact that as a business they were selling 40-pound bags of dog food at (or below) cost and shipping them for free. The business-Thinking was breaking down all along the way. In the long run, it might have been cheaper for Pets.com to have customers ship their pets to them, feed the pets there, and then ship them home. The goal is to become more aware of what assumptions are present, and make better choices about when and how to question them.

The Questions You Never Ask

Often a question forms in your mind and, for whatever reason, you don't ask it. You then have to guess about the answer. Rather than guessing (often about critical information), you need both the courage and the consideration to ask the question.

For instance, someone on the executive team may say, "You should probably know that the budget amount for this project is very limited." Have you heard a response like: "Great. Thanks for letting us know. That shouldn't be a problem because we really scrubbed this one down." And what hasn't been asked? What that limited budget amount *is!* The limited budget might be more than you ever imagined. So, you go ahead and guess about what the executive team is willing and able to spend, and they guess about how much they will need to invest. Neither party will usually find out anything concrete until after spending a lot of time scoping the project, doing the research, and preparing a presentation and proposal. And by then, if your guesses are far apart (and they probably will be), you may have grossly wasted everybody's time.

Mutual Understanding
or Mutual Mystification?

It is fascinating, and disheartening, to watch businesspeople make presentations to their decision-making colleagues when the decision makers' criteria for making the decision are unknown to the presenters.

I (Steve) worked for a company where I was a new member of a product review board. Anyone in the company who had an idea for a product was required to present a business case. It didn't have to be that complete, just a rough business case. I remember one particular meeting where someone with an idea patiently waited his turn. The board was behind schedule (as usual). When it was his turn, he handed out his business case to all the committee members, and started going through every detail. Suddenly, one of the senior committee members stood up and said, "Everything here makes a good business case for us *internally,* but it seems like you've made a big assumption that clients even want this product. All of these numbers make perfect sense *if*—and I think it's a big *if*—clients want this in the first place. My question to you is, *do they?*"

The presenter paused for a moment, and then again tried to defend his case by using the same numbers. What he was really missing was the fact that he had made two assumptions—that the market would want the product and that he understood the board's decision-making criteria. And maybe he did, but he chose to ignore them. Either way, what the committee was interested in, first and foremost, was *market need,* not profitability and project plans based on a bunch of guesses focused on internal efficiencies, and this guy was doing some major-league guessing. In his defense, he was typical in an organization of guessers who were making their first attempts to correct their course and stop guessing, and this committee wanted no more guessing. I talked to him after the meeting, and he said, "Next time I'm going to wear a bullet-proof vest!" No vest needed if you've done your businessThinking and tested your assumptions along the way, know what people expect, and are prepared.

For some reason, it seems that many people try to get buy-in on a project or approval of a solution by presenting the criteria that make the most sense to them, rather than finding out what would make the most sense to the people who will allocate the funds or be affected by the solution. Please, we beg you, never make a presentation or proposal to people whose criteria for judging your presentation are unknown to you. To do so would be immense guessing, and you are trying to maintain a relationship of mutual understanding, not mutual mystification. In other words, *no guessing!*

Much of the discipline to be followed in great businessThinking is in listening to the questions forming in your mind, and then finding a high-XQ way to ask them. Even if it seems inappropriate or uncomfortable to you, if your intent is aligned with that of your colleagues, and your ego is checked, *ask the question!* As we move forward with businessThinking, we will point out the places where no guessing applies.

Now, just because the understanding is mutual, and you're not making assumptions, that doesn't mean the *proposed* event will actually qualify as a *real* solution, so you have another move to make to keep businessThinking.

CHAPTER SEVEN

Resist the Solution Seduction!

When someone brings up a solution to a problem, or an idea to capitalize on a new opportunity, your first step is to gain mutual understanding of what it is. Once you have mutual understanding, make the counterintuitive business move with a simple, habit-breaking, tradition-destroying, convention-bending step:

 Move off the solution!

When you hear a "solution," respect it, but let it go. Resist the seductive temptation to focus any discussion on the solution itself. To avoid premature solutions, you must be made of solution-resistant material. Hold on for the bigger, better marshmallow. If you can resist the temptation to jump on the first idea or suggestion (yours or theirs), and can identify and explore all the relevant issues that are really needed to define the solution, you'll get much better thinking and avoid the *coulds*. In essence, by doing this you're moving off of a potential *could* onto the underlying business issues that would make it (or not make it) a *should*. You're probably saying, "That's it? After all the buildup, that's it?" Yes, and it's worth repeating.

Rule 3, "Move Off the Solution," gets you to the underlying business issues that need to be addressed through any solution by bringing clarity and definition to the issues, and then focusing attention on the vital few.

Moving off the solution is the first crucial move, and a counterintuitive one. Moving off the solution may not seem revolutionary. If you could move off easy, early solutions, it *would* be revolutionary. In moving off the solution, your first task is to recognize that you are, in fact, on a solution; that what you and others are hearing, seeing, or talking about is a solution—reports, campaigns, strategies, goals, meetings, research, initiatives: Whatever it is, it's an intended solution—and at this point, it may be only an event. The key is to recognize it for what it is: a ticket to the solution amusement park.

You can't let fake solutions hang around until they become familiar, get a lot of press time from everyone adopting "companyspeak," and, once they are familiar or famous, slowly get funded without the solid, critical thinking needed for exploration. What's driving your move off the solution is an intense curiosity about what the solution is trying to address. The tricky part is *recognizing* the solution when you hear it or see it. So stay aware, and when you recognize a solution, restate the solution you believe has been offered to make sure everyone hears it (and that you've got it right). Here's how you structure the curiosity and move off the solution:

1. Move off the solution and make a list of the underlying business issues the intended solution is meant to address.

2. Make sure the list of issues is complete.

3. Prioritize the list, and tackle the issues in order of priority.

Imagine you're in discussion with the marketing division about strategies to grow your market share, and someone makes the following suggestion:

Colleague: I think we need to move aggressively to develop an e-commerce Web site. If we don't, we'll lose market share that will be almost impossible to regain.

businessThink: An e-commerce Web site sounds like it could be a really good idea. Before we talk specifically about a Web site, what are the issues we're hoping to address by creating one?

Before pouring fuel on the fire by suggesting other solutions that support or reinforce the suggested idea, redirect the discussion by restating the proposed solution. Practice your responses until they are second nature. The magic is in the ability to hear a solution and move off to make a list of business issues. Once you're off the solution, you don't need a lot of description in order to identify the issues. One or two concise sound bites will work for each. Identify the issues as quickly as you can until you feel the list is fairly exhaustive. Try to keep the list to things that are highly relevant, not mildly related. For example:

Colleague: I think we need to implement a companywide project-management software system.

businessThink: That could definitely be a big need here. With the recent downsizing, that's probably a great idea. At a high level, what are all of the issues you hope project-management software would address?

With patience and discipline, you may get a list that looks something like this:

- Missed deadlines
- Increased development costs
- Low morale
- Improved time to market
- Standard approach and language for managing projects
- Unhappy customers

Make Sure the List Is Complete

In identifying the business issues, you want to make sure the list of underlying business issues is complete before you dive into any one particular issue. You might check to make sure it's complete by saying something like this:

businessThink: Let's take a look at the list of issues we have. If we could make major progress against these goals, and nothing else, would we have a real solution, or is anything missing?

If they have other ideas, you add them to the list. You will often find that one of the *last* issues added to the list is actually the most important issue on the list. It takes a while for people's minds to engage a subject, so be patient in letting the issues unfold until the list is complete. Better to exercise patience now than have a vital issue rise up later, only to wipe out the investment and the project. It is hard to wait. Balance your need for speed with patience. If you aren't patient, and don't get a complete list, you run two risks:

- You will end up using valuable time and energy talking about an issue that is not the most critical business issue. You also might be duped into thinking it *is* the most important issue.

- Even if you finally make your way to the most important issue, you will have wasted time and money getting there (and you may not get the time and money back to discuss it again). If you do get a second chance, the cost of not solving the issues will have grown.

Prioritize the Issues

Next, choose what you think is the most important, vital issue on that list. (Be careful here—ego may lead you to dominate the selection of the primary issue.) In a group, the dynamics of choosing the most important issue become a bit more challenging. Here's an idea:

1. Make sure your list of issues is exhaustive, and each issue is mutually exclusive. If they are not, combine similar issues.

2. Divide the total number of issues on the list by three. The resulting number is equal to the number of votes each person will have to allocate to select the most important issue(s).

3. As you read through the list, ask each person to vote on the issues they see as most important. For example, consider a list of 16 issues. Each person would be given five votes. As you read through the list, each person may give all five votes to one issue, or they may divide the votes among multiple issues. By the way, voting doesn't guarantee your choice is correct, just that you can agree as a group.

After the vote, it will be easy to identify the top one or two issues.

The bigger the decision, and the more complex the issues, the less likely it will be that you can tackle the issues in one session.

Even if you have the time, your brain may not have the juice to do the discussion justice. If you start talking about one issue and it absorbs many others, that's natural. If issues combine or divide or change importance, that's what the discussion is for. It's a dynamic, not static, list.

Fixed Minds, Immovable Solutions

Sometimes people won't move off the solution, and they are firmly entrenched in what they think is the next course of action to take. If they won't move, where do you go? What if you're in an egotistical, autocratic organization where decisions come down from on high and you simply implement the decisions? You get stuck between a rock and a rock—it's no fun, and it's real. There is a difference between someone saying, "I think we need to launch a new branding strategy" and "We are going to repaint our vans." In the latter case, they have already decided on the solution and only want help implementing it. Their choice may be wrong, but it is *made.*

They don't want to move off the solution or even discuss it. In essence, they say: "I've made my decision. Do you want to play or not?" You can still provide value and attempt to find a meaningful use for the immovable solution by eliciting their *criteria* for making a decision. You businessThink around two topics:

- Their criteria for the ideal solution
- Their criteria for the ideal implementation

In the preceding example, you could start out with: "Given that you know you're going to repaint the delivery vans, what would be your criteria for the perfect *motif* of the new brand?" You get out a complete list of the issues (criteria) and make sure it's complete. You could also ask, "What will be most important to you in terms of the *people* we work with?" You then proceed to businessThink, however loosely, around those criteria as well. Later, you could tie this discussion in with getting evidence, calculating impact, looking at constraints, and exploring the ripple effect.

For another quick example of businessThinking when you're stuck with a solution, if the issue were service, do you have evidence of poor service in the past or present? What was the impact of getting bad service? In the future, how would you know with certainty you were getting exactly what you wanted? What milestones would let you know you were on track? What specific measurements are you going to use? (If none exist, would those measurements be important? Do you need help setting the measurements up?) What would be the real payoff to the project and the company if you got truly superior service? Who or what else would good or bad service affect? What has stopped you from getting excellent service in the past?

In essence, if you have no choice on the solution, make sure you give it every chance you can to succeed. If it succeeds, great. If not, at least it won't be because of lazy thinking on how to implement the solution—it was just the *wrong* solution. To make the right business decision, to build a relevant, concrete, killer solution, you will deepen your understanding of the issues by gathering evidence.

The businessThink Mirror

In the following test, read each statement and check the box that best describes you. Even though the statements are focused specifically on you, ask the same questions of your department, division, management or executive team, and company.

The businessThink Solution Test

	I'm off the solution	Mediocre	Marshmallow eater
1. I concentrate on high-leverage, business-enhancing activities, and aggressively reject premature solution distractions.	❏	❏	❏
2. I aggressively manage my attention to stay focused on key initiatives and brutally eliminate activities that are not on focus.	❏	❏	❏
3. I only talk about particular solutions and make decisions after I understand what is relevant and strategic to what we are trying to accomplish as a business.	❏	❏	❏
4. When discussing business needs, I bring out *all* of the relevant business issues from myself and my colleagues, before we talk about any *one* issue.	❏	❏	❏
5. I identify the highest-leverage issues that impact our business—that is, I make a distinction between the business issues that are most relevant to our company and issues that are merely mildly related.	❏	❏	❏
6. I clarify people's use of words and phrases that may not have precise or shared meanings.	❏	❏	❏

RULE 4

Get Evidence

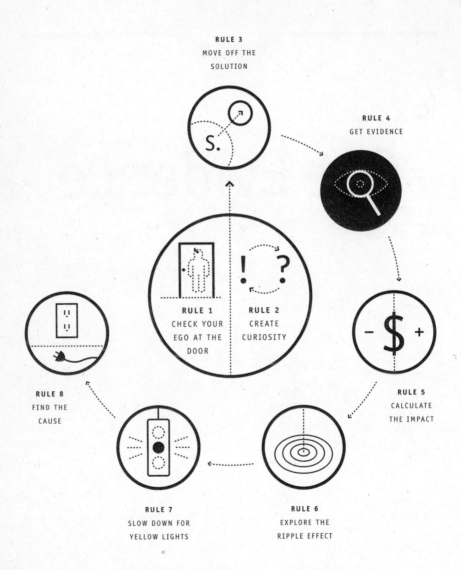

RULE 3
MOVE OFF THE
SOLUTION

RULE 4
GET EVIDENCE

S.

RULE 1
CHECK YOUR
EGO AT THE
DOOR

RULE 2
CREATE
CURIOSITY

RULE 8
FIND THE
CAUSE

RULE 5
CALCULATE
THE IMPACT

RULE 7
SLOW DOWN FOR
YELLOW LIGHTS

RULE 6
EXPLORE THE
RIPPLE EFFECT

Everybody is preaching the need for speed—the pure business adrenaline of "Internet time" or "business at the speed of thought" or "buckle up, yer goin' for a ride" speed. The idea that speed is always, absolutely, unconditionally necessary is being mentally and emotionally superglued to your brain. We offer one piece of advice to everyone currently inhabiting the lightning-express universe: *Slow down!* To businessThink, slow down long enough to get evidence.

> **Every decision is on trial. If it doesn't go to trial with you first, it will definitely be on trial when you take it to the rest of the company, or when it hits the marketplace. Before you go to trial, you need a compelling case, with evidence that the problem or opportunity you *believe* needs a solution actually *does* need a solution.**

If you don't have evidence, there is no reason to do anything—*period*. Without valid data, accurate and complete assessment of problems or opportunities becomes virtually impossible. You must look for practical illustrations of evidence that tell you if something is real, bona fide. Evidence says, "Oh yeah? Show me. Prove it!" Of course, you say it with much higher XQ and with the right intent, but that's the essence. If it's true that you will eventually take action on your decisions, then your thinking better find the evidence that proves both that you should take action, and what specific action you should take. No one will care about a fast, irrelevant solution.

Getting Evidence will give you the tools to get proof that a problem or an opportunity in fact exists, and to get a clear understanding of what it looks like, or will look like in the future. For each priority issue, you will collect soft evidence, then convert the soft evidence into hard evidence that the business can measure. It's the next critical step in helping you define whether something is a *could* or a *should* and go on to build a solid business case.

CHAPTER EIGHT

Failure at the Speed of Light: Addicted to Speed

The consulting firm of McKinsey and Company recently studied 80 Internet companies—the biggest dealers of speed—to find out just how much speed to market helped those companies succeed:

> Speed was an advantage for only 10 percent of them, and only when certain conditions were present. For the rest, moving too quickly presented no discernable advantage and resulted in wasted resources, missed opportunities, and flawed strategies.[1]

Wasted resources. Missed opportunities. Flawed strategies. Well—at least it was fast. Solutions (and companies) created in the vacuum of speed can be abandoned nearly as fast as they were sucked in.

When you ask people in business about the speed of decisions, 4 out of 5 managers and professionals say that the number of decisions they have to make is at an all-time high, and that they miss opportunities because they don't make decisions fast enough.[2] These are the same managers whose decision-making confidence is in the ninetieth percentile, and whose decisions fail half of the time. Despite the downside of absolute speed, people wish they could decide faster than a speeding bullet.

More! Faster! Panic!

In recent times, people appear to have developed the groove for speed exceptionally well. It seems there are three major buttons you are programmed and incited to hit and hit hard in the business world. Promotions are conditional on the speed and proficiency with which you can incessantly pound these buttons:

MORE

FASTER

PANIC

Each of us has spent pressured time under the typical scenario. You probably know it well, and it plays out something like this: The first quarter of the new fiscal year begins, and leaders and managers rally the troops to deliver the big "you can do it, we're the best, this is a great company" speech. They forecast their fantasies and everyone gets jazzed (or at least acts like it). People work hard, tamper with systems, do training, attempt team building, overcommunicate, talk the talk of accountability, yada, yada, yada. The first month of the next quarter comes, and in spite of all the hype, the results are less than stellar.

Now it gets serious. Everyone, especially management, starts pressing the ⊞ button. "We *really* need more! We need to work smarter, faster, do more with less. . . ."

The next month rolls in and the results are a teensy, weensy bit better, but not by much. Leaders and managers see what they want to see and grab on to the "teensy, weensy" part. "Aha. It's starting to work! It's time to turn up the heat, build some momentum, and crank those numbers!"

They quickly ignore the ⊞ button and repeatedly pound the ⏩ button with gusto. The third month's numbers come in and everyone is stunned: "We've lost ground! How could that be?!"

That's all it takes for everyone, especially management, to freak out and hit the ✵ button—and hold it down. They give more speeches, public and private (mostly private), and warn of possible layoffs, downsizing, restructuring, reanything. They cut budgets. They lean on the sales organization with large doses of pressure, and chase the pressure with a new, bold incentive program.

As you watch this state-of-the-art button pounding go on and on and on, the only discernable difference you notice from one company to the next is how many times they hit the **+** and **»** buttons before they resort to the **❋** button with an atomic elbow. The **❋** button causes *shift* to happen. People shift into high gear and get *moving*. And if you didn't know how the word *business* was spelled, and you were from planet Mars and were peering in through the windows of many companies, you could easily be persuaded that it was "*busyness*"—massive amounts of stuff getting done at hyperspeed. They're hyped, panicked, and stuck in one gear: sixth!

> **Reflection doesn't take anything away from decisiveness, from being a person of action. In fact, it generates the inner toughness that you need to be an effective person of action—to be a leader.**
> **—PETER KOESTENBAUM, BUSINESS PHILOSOPHER[3]**

Chill out! People say it all the time, but what do we all think it means? If you're really uptight, you usually see relaxing as something you do *later*, when you're away from work—on vacation or weekends. So, the other 95 percent of your life is spent uptight, wired, and under pressure? Why does business always have to be so damn *serious?* Step back a little bit. Can't you have a little more *fun?* Most people make better decisions when they're relaxed and at ease (blood actually flows to the brain better when you are relaxed), not when there is self-imposed, or other-imposed, undue pressure. Dr. Richard Carlson wrote a book titled *Don't Sweat the Small Stuff . . . and It's All Small Stuff.* Relax. Lighten up. Settle down. Lie down before you hurt yourself (or someone else).

Remember, the age-old adage isn't
"Measure once, cut 27 times." Slow down a little.
Measure twice, cut once.

How about adding a THINK! button or even a HOW? button as a balance to the corporate attention deficit disorder (ADD) of ⊞ , ⟫ and ✳ ? We'll say it again: *Slow down!* We know this prescription is going to make us seem antiquated, unhip, and out of touch. Hang with us for a minute.

> Indecision and endless discussion of every possibility on the planet (attention *surplus* disorder), with zero tolerance for even a hint of ambiguity or risk, can dilute and kill great ideas. "Measure 27 times and never cut" is just as stupid.

Daring to slow down in an impatient, "only the paranoid survive" world can seem like an enormous risk. We're not saying that speed is bad, nor is it the great, unrecognized force of evil in the world. In fact, it's one of the major outcomes of great business-Thinking. We're just asking for the occasional "speed bump" to think through what it is we're about to attach the lightning to. We're also not advocating endless banter and debate. The opposite of speed is equally lethal. Most companies have plenty of folklore that reminds everyone to be aware of "analysis paralysis," and so you become paranoid about anything that doesn't feel like action and execution. If your instinct is to think everything through to intended perfection, then you are definitely dead.

> *There is a dangerous mismatch between the amount of decision making that you have to do . . . and the speed at which an answer is required.*
> —Alvin Toffler, author of *Futureshock*[4]

The Fast Eat the Slow?

In pursuit of a fast solution, the addiction to speed makes you less discriminating about the stuff it is you're doing as long as you are in fact *doing* something—*anything*. That's why events can feel like solutions, because activity is disguised as solving and creating. Sometimes you convince yourself (and others) that if you're not "doing" at the speed of light, you must not be adding value, or you're not an A player. If everyone is racing around executing on all the *coulds,* so what, and who cares? Everyone would care if they knew, but they're too busy to know. As long as the RPMs are high enough, they can't (or don't) distinguish the *coulds* from the *shoulds,* and the enemy of the best (shoulds) becomes the fast and easy (coulds). Nobody cares about fast, flawlessly executed, irrelevant solutions. The fast, fake solution *becomes* a new problem (how ironic) and compounds the impact of the original problem, or cleverly disguises the real opportunity that you now have missed.

> **It's not the fast that eat the slow, or even the big that eat the small. It's the smart that eat the stupid!**

With all due respect to the ancient, revered proverb "Ready. Fire. Aim," it will result in shooting the business right in the _____ (choose your term).

Sucked In and Spit Out

McKinsey and Company's study on speed cites one company, a major U.S. retailer, that decided to move into e-tailing. After the company failed to attract many customers to the Web site, they decided to rapidly revamp the site and repromote it. The addiction to speed was clear: The company's leadership stated that the "decision to outsource order fulfillment for its Web site is a short-term move to . . . fulfill a need for speed." The result? Problems with order fulfillment, design, functionality, and a near-bottom ranking among 50 competing e-tailers. With the CEO of speed now out, the *new* CEO describes their current strategy as "a marathon and not a sprint."[5]

> *Getting focused on outcomes is one thing.*
> *Figuring out which outcomes are right*
> *is something else entirely.*
> —Marcus Buckingham and Curt Coffman,
> *First Break All the Rules*[6]

Just businessThink It

In breaking the addiction to speed, know what kind of race you're in: Maybe it *is* a sprint, and maybe it's a marathon. Understand the race first. If you feel pressured to make a fast decision and can't think of anything better, that doesn't mean you've found the right solution; it may mean that you need more time to think. If a decision on a particular issue has been postponed repeatedly, it may be because the business issues are still not well defined, or the problem isn't that big of a deal. Rather than forging ahead while feeling nagging uncertainty, go back to the business issues that you are trying to deal with. Get off the solution and talk about the underlying issues. Racing to the wrong solution isn't worth the fuel it takes. Switch gears.

Before you launch into solutions, shift from the "just do it" mentality to a "just businessThink it" mentality. Speed needs conscious placement and careful balance when creating solutions. You definitely need speed, but at the right RPM and at the appropriate time. The timing of the speed, and the absolute speed itself, are both critical. Slow down long enough to make sure that what you're doing is relevant, concrete, clear, and leveraged for the business. Learn to embrace a few incisive question marks before engraving the exclamation points of the solution in stone. Then you can bring in all the exclamation points you want!!! Your bias for action will be given a welcomed return, and you will definitely focus and execute. Replace absolute speed with *businessThink* speed.

If you've been businessThinking, you have your ego checked; you've moved off the solutions to the real issues, and you've prioritized those issues. The next shift you make in businessThinking is to get evidence. Evidence tells you if something worth prevention or invention even exists for the list of priority business issues you've captured. Before you learn to collect evidence, let's talk about the *reason* you get evidence and what turns up when you finally do, in the following chapter.

The businessThink Mirror

In the following test, read each statement and check the box that best describes you. Even though the statements are focused specifically on you, ask the same questions of your department, division, management or executive team, and company.

The businessThink Speed Test

	Yes	Sometimes	Panic
1. Before taking action, I consider roughly how much money we are really losing every day we don't decide or take action.	❏	❏	❏
2. I pause to ask the question, "Is the need for speed justified and real?" And if it is, how?	❏	❏	❏
3. I examine whether the need for speed is merely to reduce our anxiety about temporary ambiguity, or if we are really getting hurt by not moving right now.	❏	❏	❏
4. I stop to consider whether this is something urgent, important, or both.	❏	❏	❏
5. I'm not driven by crisis; I consider everything in context of priorities.	❏	❏	❏
6. I try to consistently evaluate the need to move fast on a particular project or decision with a corporate strategy that needs the speed.	❏	❏	❏
7. I don't often feel pressured, or pressure myself, to make a decision fast.	❏	❏	❏
8. Not being able to think of anything better is not an excuse to just plow ahead.	❏	❏	❏
9. When I take action, if I feel any uncertainty, I slow down and think it through before I move ahead.	❏	❏	❏
10. Looking busy isn't how people value the work we do.	❏	❏	❏
11. When project dates and deadlines are established, they are based on objective criteria and are not chosen arbitrarily.	❏	❏	❏

CHAPTER NINE

In God We Trust—
Everyone Else Bring
Evidence

Here's a quick metaphor that shows why, and how, you start the search for evidence. It comes from generations of TV cop shows—*NYPD Blue, Law & Order, Dragnet, Adam-12, Starsky and Hutch* (now we're showing our age)—take your generational pick. In the older shows, it usually started with a call from headquarters dispatching the police to the scene: "One Adam-12, One Adam-12, see the man. . . ." When the police arrived at the crime scene, what was one of the first things they looked for? As Joe Friday would say, "Just the facts, Ma'am. Just the facts." In other words— evidence! Police don't start grabbing anyone in the vicinity and hauling them in as suspects (well, at least the good ones don't). The first rule in working a crime scene is to *find* (not plant) evidence that leads to the suspects, *not* the other way around.

If detectives begin the investigation by scrambling for suspects, and don't rope off the scene first, the evidence can disappear. Sometimes the evidence is easy to see, and they simply miss it. Seldom is the easy evidence alone sufficient to give them reason to detain or convict suspects. Easy evidence is often misleading and not as convincing as someone with an untrained eye might think.

Those with expertise frequently dig a little deeper to see what they missed at first glance. Good detectives don't conclude the search until they are confident they have gathered sufficient evidence to put the pieces together. The more pieces they get, the clearer the picture. The clearer the picture, the more likely the conviction from a judge or jury.

There are crime scenes in business, too. You get a call or a memo, it's a code red, and you get briefed on the problem. Of course, you are paid to solve problems, so you jump hard and fast to get a team of experts involved. You race to the scene (probably a meeting). After quickly surveying the scene, you run around the streets (halls) looking for as many suspects (vendors and colleagues) as possible to solve the crime (problem). You see many suspects, get excited, and decide to detain (retain) a few. In doing so, you break the first rule of investigation:

Get Evidence—collect evidence or proof that you could do something, and then convert soft evidence into measurable hard evidence.

> The real purpose of the scientific method is to make sure Nature hasn't misled you into thinking you know something you actually don't know.
> **—R. PIRSIG, *ZEN AND THE ART OF MOTORCYCLE MAINTENANCE*[1]**

But too often, people don't get evidence.

> *When you fail to see the reality that*
> *your solution will be on trial, you don't*
> *get a conviction; you get a mistrial.*

When you go to trial to present your proposed solution to get funding without evidence, the judge and jury (colleagues with strong, objective business rationales) throw out the case. Don't be so anxious to solve the crime of the century that you miss the key evidence and end up unprepared for trial.

But suppose a proposed idea sneaks by, under cover, and without evidence, and the check-writing jury funds your solution. (Unfortunately, it happens.) Isn't it likely that someone, at some point, is going to stand up and say "Can someone please prove to me why we needed to do this in the first place?" Or later, "So what's different now after we have spent all this money?" Hindsight won't bring the wasted money back. How will anyone be able to judge success if there is no baseline of evidence to begin with and no evidence of success in the end? Ask and answer those questions yourself now before others do it for you later.

If you don't, you may have to live with some of the downsides:

- Premature discussion about a solution's features and benefits is mistaken for evidence.
- There isn't objective rationale or criteria for funding solutions.
- Discerning the *coulds* from the *shoulds* becomes nearly impossible.
- There is no measure for defining or judging success.
- Divergent perspectives and unique viewpoints are missed.
- Conversion of the idea into financial impact is lost.

> We humans seem to be extremely good at generating ideas, theories and explanations that have the ring of plausibility. We may be relatively deficient, however, in evaluating and testing our ideas once they are formed.
> —THOMAS GILOVICH, *HOW WE KNOW WHAT ISN'T SO*[2]

The Soft and the Hard

The purpose of the pursuit of evidence is to get people to open their minds and their mouths and talk about what leads you or them to believe something *is* a problem; to verify that the problem *really* exists. In your pursuit of evidence, it is important to remember that not all evidence is created equal. Since business evidence is *knowledge,* not physical evidence at a crime scene, you need to communicate in depth about the most important business issues to collect the evidence. When you dig for evidence on the most important issues, once you've moved off the solution, you are looking for a description of what *has* happened or *will* happen that will convince you to continue your pursuit of a solution. As you arrive on the scene to uncover evidence, there are basically two levels of evidence to look for (Table 9.1):

- *Level 1: Soft evidence.* Descriptive, circumstantial, anecdotal, subjective, qualified data.
- *Level 2: Hard evidence.* Measured, validated, objective, quantified data.

Table 9.1   Levels of Evidence

Level 1: Soft Evidence	Level 2: Hard Evidence
People seem confused about organizational priorities.	Our *productivity* is off significantly.
There is *no teamwork* in our department.	*Product defects* and returns are rising.
People don't trust management.	We are *losing customers.*
Our *salespeople complain* they don't have remote access when they are on the road.	The cross-selling *conversion rate* is not what we want it to be.
We need *more collaboration* and *better communication* between divisions.	*Speed to market* has dropped off.
Our *brand is weakening.*	Our *market share* has eroded over the last three quarters.
Morale is low and the company culture is negative.	*Turnover is up* over last year.
We need *coaching and training reinforcement.*	*Customer satisfaction* is dropping.
Our *products and services are undervalued.*	We need to improve our *gross margin percentage.*
Management doesn't trust us.	*New product development* has dropped off.
We are top-heavy and bureaucratic.	*Selling, general, and administrative expenses* are too high.
We lack *strategic direction.*	*Net profit* has dropped.

Search for the Soft

Soft evidence is the subjective, anecdotal, qualified layer of data on top, and *hard evidence* is the quantified, measured, validated foundation or bedrock beneath. Because not all evidence is created equal, there is a reason evidence is in this sequence. The first level of soft evidence is the easiest to find and most common. Most people can safely and quickly give you evidence from their own experience, from what they have seen or observed, even if it is happening only in their department or division. They will tell you stories or give you "word on the street" instances of evidence. Soft evidence allows for divergent opinions (usually theirs), unique perspectives (usually theirs), and a local, functional sense of what is going on (according to them).

Usually, a healthy amount of soft evidence naturally leads to the deeper, second level—*hard evidence.* Soft evidence, without the validation and verification of hard evidence, can deceive people into thinking they have done their homework and that they are actually solving something. Nobody ends up having to prove anything, and so many ideas get funded irrationally. Ultimately, you're digging and drilling for hard evidence.

Dig for the Hard

Hard evidence is measured or verified data, and is harder to find. In every organization, there are things that are important to the business that are regularly measured. These can be goals or targets against which people are often expected to perform, and they are frequently operational in nature. They commonly show up in the company's strategic initiatives, in profit-and-loss statements, or on a corporate scorecard. Hard evidence is the most powerful form of evidence because it leads to the impact on the business and its people, and every effort should be made to state the impact in financial terms that relate to the strategies and performance of the company. Money will become the acid test that moves *could* to the Holy Grail of *should.* It's important to turn all nonfinancial measures into financial impact, and the impact will be either big or small. If the impact is small, so what, and who cares? You should stop everything—now.

> *The cost of the solution may be bigger than the cost of the problem or opportunity.*

If the impact is big enough to care about, then it probably warrants spending your time to build a killer solution.

A Predictable Path

When looking for and gathering soft or hard evidence, you either have it or you don't (even we were able to figure that one out). When talking to people, it is surprising to find that even when they are intimately connected to the issues, they often can't come up with the evidence, or their evidence is soft. This is not as surprising when you're talking with people who are less connected to the problem. If the evidence exists in the organization, and you don't have it personally, find out who has it and when you can get it. If you don't have the evidence, or if it *doesn't* exist, you need to determine whether it's important to have it. If the evidence *is* important, can you get it on your own, or do you need some help? If you do need help, who can help you get it?

Where Is It?

When you look for evidence, it comes from one of two places— *inside* the company, or *outside* the company (we're on a roll). In considering both sources of evidence, you'll need to carefully think through the evidence and see how relevant it is to your case. Is it highly relevant or just mildly related? Opinions will differ. That's why you do this stuff. You'll make the right decision more often if you have both inside *and* outside evidence. Depending on the type of decision, if it's more internally or externally focused, you'll rely on one type of evidence more than the other. And you will be more confident if both the inside *and* outside evidence you gather is both soft *and* hard.

It's very common for hard evidence to be found outside your company. For example, you might read some hard, well-researched information on your market from Accenture. Or you might attend an industry conference and hear a keynote speaker quote some research regarding worker productivity being down 15 percent. Or perhaps you or others might be talking to a peer at another company that's struggling with a similar issue, and some information is shared. Maybe you subscribe to an industry newsletter or trade magazine where some research or data is presented.

Outside evidence is tempting because it is so abundantly available and seems more convenient. Rather than digging for it yourself, you just rely on the experience of others. The danger of outside evidence is that it may be valid and reliable research, it may sound compelling, and it may or may not apply to your business. When it comes to outside evidence, people frequently presume that the situation in their own company is at the extremes— much worse or much better than average. Once you've read something that leads you to believe that the outside evidence applies to you, and armed with this data in mind, you might make some general observations as you walk around and talk with people. Sometimes that leads you to believe the evidence is admissible and relevant.

Inside evidence often comes from observation, word on the street, or talk over lunch; it consists of soft or anecdotal information, stories, and the like. It is also possible that you may have done some research in your own firm. You know it applies because you did it yourself. The danger is that many times this "research" is not research at all, but an exercise that serves as validation to entrench a predetermined position driven by biases, ego, and hidden agendas. It is evidence gathered with the intent of supporting rather than illuminating—of bolstering a position rather than revealing proof. A common mistake is to use soft evidence from inside your company to validate hard evidence that comes from outside the company. Even though it's tempting to think you have enough evidence, push yourself to go one step farther and gather hard evidence inside your company.

Imagine you're creating a new product for the outside world, maybe for a new market. The danger of using inside evidence exclusively is that it reflects only your company, your opinion, and it may not be validated by the market when tested. It becomes a painful and expensive lesson when people outside your company don't accept the solution. Test inside evidence against outside evidence.

Because soft evidence leads to hard evidence, let's go on to the next chapter and start with the search for soft evidence.

The businessThink Mirror

In the following test, read each statement and check the box that best describes you. Even though the statements are focused specifically on you, ask the same questions of your department, division, management or executive team, and company.

The businessThink Evidence Test

	Yes	Now and then	I am the antisleuth
1. When someone brings up a problem, I help find or think through the information that proves the problem exists.	❏	❏	❏
2. When someone says that they want a particular result, I get a clear understanding of how we will know we achieved the result.	❏	❏	❏
3. I ask people what they think, and find value in their responses, even if it's just their opinion.	❏	❏	❏
4. I get enough soft and hard evidence to get a conviction before I go to trial and propose a solution for a problem or opportunity.	❏	❏	❏
5. Even though outside evidence may be compelling, I check to make sure it's relevant and that it applies to my company.	❏	❏	❏
6. Even though inside evidence may be compelling, I test it with outside sources to see if it's accurate and complete.	❏	❏	❏

• CHAPTER TEN •

Searching for Soft Evidence

We could try to make this sound complex, but it's really simple:

Rule 4: Get Evidence.   Collect evidence or proof that you could do something, and convert soft evidence into measurable hard evidence.

> **Soft evidence is the first businessThink filter for ideas. If it doesn't make it through the soft-evidence filter, it's over. If you don't have evidence, there is no reason to move forward—*period*. Although getting soft evidence is simple, it's often ignored.**

Here's a case in point. One of our friends works as a senior manager for a large travel company. A colleague of his (the CEO) decided to announce the launch of a new product brand. The initiative was launched before any of the company's senior directors or managers had a chance to buy in to the concept. It was announced to the company and presented, somewhat covertly, to the board of directors as a way to grow the business. The decision was made with no feasibility study; not an ounce of market

127

research or evidence. No determination of how it fit into the company's overall strategy. No search for soft evidence or discussion with colleagues or customers. No thought to what might stop it from succeeding. Basically, no thought.

The CEO was so determined to make this happen that when the team of directors listed over 30 reasons why the new product was doomed to fail, he turned around and said, "Well, we've announced it to the company, so we have to execute it. Besides, no one here has brought me any new ideas of how to grow the business, and this is what I came up with. We just need to execute and make my idea successful."

The product has since been killed and revived several times—hundreds of thousands of dollars in opportunity lost, thousands of hours wasted on justifying and resuscitating the project, and morale depleted. Without evidence, there is no reason to move—unless, of course, you have an ego the size of Godzilla and the political clout to force it through.

The quickest way to find soft evidence is to *ask* for it—invite people to describe what they have seen, heard, felt, and experienced. No bright lights of interrogation needed. With soft evidence, the devil is in the details, so search closely. Henry Mintzberg, one of the leading thinkers on strategy in the world, has some great thoughts on this. Here's one of them:

> *While hard data may inform our intellect, it is largely soft data that generates wisdom. . . . Hard information is often limited in scope, lacking richness, and often fails to encompass important non-economic and non-quantitative factors.*
> —Henry Mintzberg, *The Rise and Fall of Strategic Planning*[1]

Ask How and What Questions

There are two simple words that will help you start to gather soft evidence: *how* and *what*. Although simple, they are not simplistic. The purpose of asking these questions is to get people to share their perspectives, and to help you understand their perspectives. It inevitably gives you a lay of the land, viewpoints, the environment; in essence, "What's going on?"

> It is not information of a general sort that helps. Not surveys, not the bland amalgams. It is the odds and ends of tangible detail that pieced together . . . illuminate the underside of issues.
>
> **–RICHARD NEUSTADT,**
> **HARVARD SCHOLAR AND ADVISER TO U.S. PRESIDENTS[2]**

Another purpose of asking these questions is to invite everyone as collective businesspeople to think through opinions and ideas to see if they hold up. If they don't hold up now, they won't hold up under hard evidence or impact. Here are some examples on a variety of topics to help you get the gist of how to ask evidence questions.

How

- *How* will we know if we improved brand loyalty?
- *How* do we know we need to reorganize?
- *How, specifically,* is poor leadership showing up?
- *How* did we become convinced client trust is eroding?
- *How, specifically,* would we measure our ability to recruit and keep top talent?

What

- *What, specifically,* will we consider success if we expand our product line?
- *What* will we observe that will let us know morale has improved?
- *What, specifically,* lets us know quality is down?
- *What* convinced us that competitors have superior services?
- *What, specifically,* makes us think we need to add an e-commerce functionality to our Web site?

The questions aren't rocket science, but it's not always easy to ask them even when they seem obvious.

> *In our observations, some of the best businesspeople ask the obvious questions, the answers to which are almost never obvious. In fact, it's the obvious questions or the politically sensitive questions that many are most afraid to ask.*

These questions may seem too simple, and people may feel the risk of sounding stupid, but these are the questions that get blown off way too much! People are paid to ask them, it's important to ask them, but they just *don't* ask them. What appears to one person to be an obvious question isn't always obvious to everyone else.

> **"Please give me an example."** These are the five most important words in the [businessperson's] arsenal, and they can't be used enough.
>
> **–TOM PETERS, *THE PURSUIT OF WOW!*[3]**

When you do ask questions and search for evidence, people will probably give you the *soft* evidence of opinions, stories, and experiences. You might hear things like the following:

- Our return policies aren't customer friendly.
- It is estimated that 70 percent of IT [information technology] projects fail to produce the expected benefits because the IT processes are not integrated into work processes. I think we're at risk.
- Salespeople don't talk to marketing.
- People aren't held accountable.
- Everyone is complaining that we don't have it (whatever *it* is).
- An article I recently read said that 14 percent of executives' time is wasted on poor communication between management and staff.
- We don't follow through on our commitments.
- We're always changing direction.
- We don't know how to manage projects around here.
- Too many people are saying one thing in the meeting, and then what they *really* think to a select few *after* the meeting.

You may also get statements and philosophies that are embedded in the company culture: "The customer is always right," "Management always wins," or "Execution is more important than strategy." Write it down. Soak it up. Make note of it. At this point, it's all admissible evidence. You want in-depth information that will help you figure this thing out. Don't measure the importance or accuracy of the evidence people give you based on the seniority of the people you ask, but rather on how close they are to the situation, and how they are impacted by the potential problem or opportunity. When looking for evidence, "juniority" can matter as much as or more than seniority.

At this point you're trying to gather enough evidence to balance individual perspectives. Sometimes people hit a mental block and run out of examples they can give to your *how* and *what* questions. Here are some additional questions you can ask to help you gather even more evidence from the same person.

Too Much or Too Little?

One minor twist on *how* and *what* questions can help you dig up more evidence: the *too much or too little* test. Ask the basic question: "What do we have too much or too little of?"

- *What* is there too little of that suggests we are not utilizing the talent of our people?

- *What* are we seeing too much of that would tell us our speed to market is down?

- *What* are we hearing too much or too little of that suggests people lack information to make the right decisions?

The essence of the *too much or too little* question basically boils down to this: If you were a fly on the wall and no one knew you were watching, what would you see *too much* or *too little* of in your company that would suggest you need a solution?

- There are too many CYA memos flying around.

- There's not enough collaboration. People are getting really frustrated.

- Too much of our time is spent focused on moving to B2B [business-to-business] e-commerce.

- I hear too many customers complaining about our service.
- We're too slow to respond to changes in the market.

Taken all together, the soft evidence you have gathered is extremely valuable, and gives you important insight.

> *Be aware that the ultimate value of evidence will be tied to how true it is, and the impact it has on the company.*

Because it is just opinion, some of what you will hear may be questionable; it's an overstatement or an understatement, and that's normal. Ask additional questions to gather more depth or specificity on what has been said. For instance, someone might say, "We absolutely have to add this [whatever *this* is] to our current offerings or we will lose business. Customers are screaming for it." There is a whole bunch of clarity missing in a statement like "People are screaming for it." For example, here's what might run through your head:

- Who, specifically, is screaming for it?
- How frequently have you heard this?
- All of them said the same thing?
- What specific functionality are we talking about?
- Do all customers feel the same way?

Ask for concrete illustrations to get past mere opinions. As you pursue the concrete and consider what people say, it becomes apparent that soft evidence is a *very* difficult thing to nail down—the cement doesn't always harden in helping you get to specific, measurable, financial impact on the business. The good news is that soft evidence provides context, often gives you quality leads to chase down, and helps people feel understood and valued. Soft evidence also usually leads to hard evidence, and that leads to impact. The bad news is that, unlike hard evidence, soft evidence is usually not from a monitored, measured occurrence. To turn bad news into good, you can turn soft evidence into hard evidence, and you do that by continuing to dig for evidence, only now you dig as deep as you can.

CHAPTER ELEVEN

Digging for Hard Evidence

So far you've been collecting evidence you can't really measure easily. Although it's useful information, it's also hard to quantify. You might find clues like these: People may say they don't feel they are getting the most out of their staff, their marketing, their strategy, or their reputation in the marketplace. They need a better plan, creative thinking, more innovation, or improved teamwork. How will you quantify the value of those issues? By converting soft evidence into hard evidence.

I (Steve) mentioned earlier that I was a partner in a firm that helped human resources and training people diagnose the training and organizational development needs of their organizations. Our ideas didn't seem to be revolutionizing our clients nor our revenue stream, so we hired a marketing research firm to analyze what our clients wanted, and to see if what the clients wanted matched what we were able and passionate to deliver.

The marketing firm asked good questions and told us that our clients passionately shared a lot of helpful information. We were excited (and relieved) because the soft evidence validated our hope that our clients wanted our products and services. We had no doubt that almost every individual who was interviewed thought what we had was valuable.

Unknowingly, we duped ourselves into thinking that because we had numbers from 20 people at 20 different companies, the data was hard, and therefore all we needed. Nothing can make soft evidence seem hard better than statistics. The problem was, we couldn't connect the evidence to something that other people in the client company could relate to as a business result that businesspeople would care about. We were talking to *human resources* people about human resources issues, and in isolation from the business issues the client companies were facing, we didn't convert the soft evidence of opinions, observations, and human resource viewpoints into hard evidence that the clients' *business* people could relate to.

> **Without hard evidence that is clear and concise about the payoff to the business, clients will often tell you what you want to hear. They will also have a hard time convincing anyone else that the company needs their ideas.**

Colleagues often tell you what they think you want to hear. That's not malicious, it's just part of human nature to be nice. Soft evidence is helpful and important—and if *left* as soft evidence, it produces soft results. The challenge is in getting to the heart of the matter, and what matters most at this point is *money*.

> *There has to be a path that leads to an economic return, or even the best of ideas are relegated to the pile of nice-to-haves (coulds), but not the imperative must-haves (shoulds).*

Before you can get directly to the money, you have to turn soft evidence into hard evidence, which will become a launching pad for impact. You will also have no evidence to calculate the impact. No impact, no reason to do anything. To make that conversion, you dig for hard evidence that proves you need a solution.

 Rule 4: Get Evidence.   Collect evidence or proof that you could do something, and *convert soft evidence into measurable hard evidence.*

Around and Down

Hard evidence takes you to the money, or impact. Your goal in digging for evidence is to move from a broad, generic description of an issue to the underlying motivation or key driver. From an XQ perspective, you move from soft to hard measures, and from that which is known, intellectual, and safe to that which is unexamined, emotional, and possibly vulnerable. You are trying to get real about what makes this important—intellectually and emotionally. If you start with a problem—something people want to remove, avoid, or move away from—then you will dig for *pain*. If you start with a result—something they want to achieve, obtain, or move toward—you will dig for *gain*.

The key discrimination to make in digging for hard evidence is the difference between going *around* a level of investigation and going *down* a level of investigation (Figure 11.1).

> **First, you can *dig around* with the questions you learned to use in gathering soft evidence: *how* and *what*. Second, you can *dig down* with questions that track down hard evidence.**

Here's the catch: Questions that dig around for soft evidence don't dig down to hard evidence. Most people get lost in going around (collecting evidence), and are either unwilling or unable to strip away enough layers to dig down to the true impact, to the heart of the matter.

Digging down is a conversational excavation toward hard evidence that shows up as a *measured* event. When you dig down you may not get to hard evidence in one swift move. It may take sev-

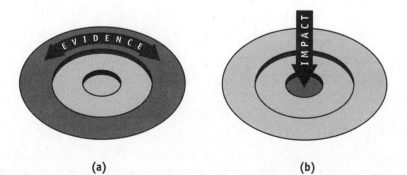

(a)   (b)

Figure 11.1   Digging for hard evidence: (a) going *around* a level of investigation, and (b) going *down* a level of investigation.

eral times before you hit the mother lode. When asking these questions, you will notice that you start to move *closer* to the next level or layer of evidence. If you ask enough times, you will eventually hit the bedrock of hard evidence. The best way to describe digging for hard evidence is to give some examples.

Digging for Gain

The key phrase when digging for hard evidence on the gain side is "What would that allow us to do that we can't do as a business today?" So you can know whether you are digging for gain, listen carefully to what people say they want. They will tell you their primary motivation through key phrases that will cue you to dig for gain. These may include things like the following:

- The objectives we are striving for are . . .
- We are looking to accomplish . . .
- Our targets in the future are . . .
- In the ideal world, . . .
- The improvements we're expecting to achieve are . . .

While you may pause to ask some soft-evidence questions along the way for context, your focus is to give them what they said they wanted by asking "What does that allow you to do that you can't do today?" You can definitely vary how you ask that question: "What does that get you?" "Where do the benefits of that show up?" "How does that impact performance?" "How does that help the bottom line?" "Best-case scenario, what will be the ultimate gain?" and so on. The key is to keep cutting away layers until you get to something that is a key business driver. Here's an example:

Colleague: What we really need here is better communication between engineering and manufacturing.

businessThink: You're probably right on. If we improved our communication, what would that allow us to do that we can't do today?

In this example, a colleague is asking for something they want (gain): improved communication. The businessThink response, rather than arguing the merits of how good the communication is already (or making any other argument for or against), tries to find out what getting what they are asking for would actually allow them to do that they can't do now.

When digging for hard evidence, you're going to hear plenty of soft evidence along the way. It's not that frequent (or that valuable) an event that someone says, "I think we need to improve morale" and someone rises up saying, "Yeah! Improving morale would decrease turnover and recruiting costs. If we could improve morale we would add $1.269 million to the bottom line. That is a multiplier of 3.5 on return on equity! Let's do it!" Saying to your colleagues, "Just give me the hard evidence—show me the money!" isn't exactly helpful in creating an open, honest environment. Digging quickly and directly isn't conducive to creating rapport or understanding the context of the situation in the grander scheme of things.

> *The simple fact that you're businessThinking doesn't grant you the God-given right to interrogate people or push (shove) their thinking. That's part of the reason it's not one swift, sweeping, lightning-fast hack for hard evidence.*

People need and deserve time to work through their thinking to gather soft *and* hard evidence, and they need to see the connection between soft and hard evidence for themselves.

In addition, this is not done to agitate people or make them feel stupid. You are digging because they have a unique perspective, and you need to eventually prove your case with the hard data, with the numbers.

Digging for Pain

Many times you're working with people who are hoping to eliminate pain. They're telling you what they don't want or where it hurts. They may even use words describing physical or emotional pain:

- It's killing us . . .
- We're bleeding . . .

- We have to correct . . .
- It is so painful when . . .
- What's hurting us is . . .
- What's stopping us is . . .
- We're concerned about . . .

Some people find it harder, more uncomfortable, to explore pain. To them, talking about the wonderful things people *do* want is easier than delving into the depths of what people *don't* want. However, because people are more often motivated to move away from pain rather than to move toward gain, and it seems that there's a lot more discussion of pain than of gain in companies, you still need to get to the core motivation and underlying business issues.

So here's how you dig down for pain. The key phrase is, "And then what happens?"

Again, you can vary that phrase in many ways: "And what does that affect?" "And what are the consequences of that?" "And what does that in turn impact?" "Worst-case scenario, if you never change this, what will happen?"

For example, if the person says, "What's really killing us is not having the right people get the right information at the right time," you cut for pain by asking, "And when the right people don't get the right information at the right time, then what happens?"

Colleague: We're not getting one holistic view of the customer when they call in, and it's killing us. (Soft evidence)

businessThink: That sounds frustrating. When we're not getting that view, then what's happening?

Colleague: Customers are getting a widely varying level of service depending on whom and where they call in the company. (Softish, but starting to sound hard, with terms like *levels of service*)

businessThink: Hmm. And because customers are getting widely varying levels of service in the organization, what's showing up?

Colleague: Customers are getting frustrated and reps are ineffective.

businessThink: This is very helpful. This may seem like an

obvious question, and if it's okay I'll ask it anyway. When our customers are frustrated and the reps' effectiveness goes down—*then what happens?*

Colleague: Our product orders are going down, costing us revenue, and we're losing reps, which means turnover costs are up.

Bam! You've hit bedrock, you have hard evidence. You don't know how strongly it will register as impact—yet. You simply know you've hit something hard that is measurable (or at least is likely to be measured). The measurable alert has gone off, and once alerted, you use a different tool to convert the evidence from hard to impact. We will get to that in the next chapter.

By the way, there are a lot of things your colleague could have said in the last answer that would have shown up as rock-solid, hard evidence. It might be different with each person you talk to, and within each individual function in your company. All you want to know for the moment is what *this* person will lead you to discover. The hard evidence that registers will be what is most important to them, and it's often something against which their performance is measured. Here are some possibilities:

- Increased staff costs
- Overtime
- Cost of rework
- Poor quality
- Competition taking market share and mind share
- Customer complaints
- Product returns

The Measurable Alert

Most organizations, even nonprofits, need to pay close attention to numbers somewhere in their business. These are things they *already* measure. If what you are considering could be measured but currently isn't, you need to continue to dig for hard evidence until you get to something that *is* measured—some hard evidence. The good news here is that every company has some form of measurables: financial measures, operational measures, performance measures, technology or process measures, scorecards, and customer sat-isfaction measures. We're not saying they are the *right* measures, nor are we saying they are *accurate.* We are saying we all *have* them. As soon as you hear hard evidence, that is when your mental meas-urable alert needs to go off.

If You Feel It, Ask It

When doing field research, we often observe that businesspeople who have been trained in finding hard evidence get close to the last level of questioning, and just before they get to the hard evi-dence or a measurable, they bail out to someplace safe, such as a solution, *before* they understand the real, bottom-line issues. After-ward, when talking with them, we ask if they could hear in their mind what the next question should have been. They usually say, "Yes, but clearly the other person would have felt uncomfortable had I asked that question."

So, being curious by nature and trying to live our own material, we go back and ask their colleague, "If they had asked this ques-tion, what would have been your reaction?"

They often say, "Tough question—but a good question, though. I would have liked to talk about that."

So, often the reason we give for not getting to the heart of the matter is that *we,* not they, would feel uncomfortable.

> The irony is that we wait to establish rapport before asking the hard question, and yet it is asking the hard question that can es-tablish rapport.

The challenge with evidence questions, although vital, is that people get lost in loads of information that don't get to the heart of the matter because they feel safe there. They forget that at some point they're going to have to have a solid business case. It's not as if people know their eventual responses, and they're just waiting for you to ask the questions so they can tell you. Often, they them-selves haven't been through the intellectual or emotional rigor of figuring out the real consequences of their problem or opportu-nity. Getting to the heart of the matter provides added value to everyone who is interested in and affected by the eventual solution. Remember the commitment to no guessing. If nobody understands the true motivation—the difference that will make a difference—then it will be difficult to get a solution that exactly meets the company's needs. If you're guessing, exactly which needs are you going to meet?

Conversion Equals Conviction

The key to cutting for hard evidence is to be dialed in to the difference between soft and hard evidence. Soft evidence will give you a flavor of what's going on; hard evidence is measured and can convince. If you were to guess (sorry to make you guess), what kind of evidence would you say most people come up with most of the time? *Soft.* Hard evidence can validate or invalidate soft evidence. As you present your business case to the jury, they will demand proof that both problems and opportunities exist, and that they have a basis in worthwhile economic return. If you can't show impact, how will you know whether you should live with a problem or do something about it?

> *Evidence gives strong information that lets you know whether you should seize the opportunity or let it pass by without a second thought.*

Sometimes the cost of the solution is more than the cost of the problem or opportunity itself.

Now that you have hard evidence, you are going to convert hard evidence into impact (and hope that it's money). Conversion equals conviction.

The businessThink Mirror

In the following test, read each statement and check the box that best describes you. Even though the statements are focused specifically on you, ask the same questions of your department, division, management or executive team, and company.

The businessThink Hard Evidence Test

	Rock solid	From time to time	Soft
1. When looking for proof of a problem or opportunity, I keep digging for evidence until I find something measurable.	❏	❏	❏
2. I regularly build a business case for any solution with both soft and hard evidence.	❏	❏	❏
3. I recognize *pain* or *gain* language when people are sharing evidence.	❏	❏	❏
4. I often help people understand their problems better than they were able to on their own, and help create a story line that makes a compelling business case.	❏	❏	❏

Calculate the Impact

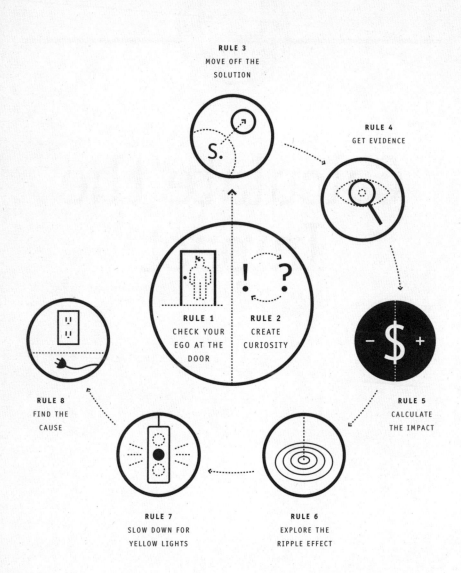

RULE 3
MOVE OFF THE
SOLUTION

RULE 4
GET EVIDENCE

S.

RULE 1
CHECK YOUR
EGO AT THE
DOOR

RULE 2
CREATE
CURIOSITY

RULE 8
FIND THE
CAUSE

RULE 5
CALCULATE
THE IMPACT

RULE 7
SLOW DOWN FOR
YELLOW LIGHTS

RULE 6
EXPLORE THE
RIPPLE EFFECT

Brace yourself for another reminder of a recurring theme: Just because you *can* do something doesn't mean you *should!* People struggle with the decision to invest in a solution—new computer systems, production facilities, a new product. What makes decisions about what new opportunities to invest in hard is not knowing how big the problem is and what the financial impact would be if it were solved. With limited resources and unlimited options, solutions will have to measure up against questions of strategic fit and stack up against other solutions. If you can't articulate the financial impact of your proposed solution to those who ultimately decide if it will be a go, you will lose the green light to something else with a clear value, even though it may provide less long-term value to your company. No matter how killer the impact of your solution, the business leaders around you won't understand it, and the company loses. When the impact is missing, any criteria (positional power, sacred cows, or political clout) can cut in and persuade people to accept inferior ideas that offer irrelevant solutions of lesser impact. Without financial clarity, nonbusinesspeople, nonbusiness cases, and nonbusiness solutions win.

> **Businesspeople never let cash out the door that doesn't strictly, ultimately, bring more cash back.**

Money Doesn't Talk, It Screams

Without the right information about the financial impact, it's not unusual for the cost of a solution to turn out to be greater than the cost of living with the problem. At the end of the day, solutions are on the line to impact the top or bottom line. If you and your colleagues can't put a worthwhile return on the investment, then the investment is simply a cost, and costs are always too high! If the impact of the problem you're analyzing or the opportunity you're considering isn't worth the money, there is no reason to move forward—*period*. Actually, *exclamation point!* If you have people, products, policies, or anything else that do nothing but generate costs, then they are draining valuable resources. They must generate some tangible financial impact or phenomenal intangible value.

Calculating the Impact will give you the tools to convert hard evidence into a ballpark financial equivalent. Once you have the impact, you can compare it against what it will cost you to put the solution into place; you will have a clear understanding of the ratio between the investment required and the return expected. Having a ballpark impact will help you make a more objective decision, and you will know whether you *could* do something or whether you absolutely *should*.

CHAPTER TWELVE

Whiteboard Economics

Most of us are not the accountants and financial wizards the traditional business world deems worthy and capable of running complex spreadsheets and forecasting hard-core numbers, so you may get uptight even talking about numbers. Sometimes you might work harder at trying to convince somebody (with passion and decibels) that you don't need the numbers than it would take to get some simple numbers in place. Without a deep knowledge of finance, the financial part of business makes us insecure about being businesspeople. Even the terms (and their abbreviations) can seem daunting—earnings before interest, tax, depreciation, and amortization (EBITDA), return on investment (ROI), time value of money, discounted cash flow analysis, average weighted cost of capital, profit and loss (P&L), RO . . . AEIOU. For businessThink, we'll strip away some of the intimidating parts of the detailed, functional expertise required to do corporate finance and accounting.

businessThink Finance 101

Our approach to businessThink Finance 101 is what we call *whiteboard* or *back-of-the-envelope* economics. We're not pretending this is rigorous financial analysis. You're grabbing the nearest white-board, notepad, or scrap paper and jotting down some rough, ball-park ideas about the size of the numbers. If somebody told you that $300 or $400 had been wasted in your department, you probably wouldn't think much of it. If they told you $300,000 or $400,000 had been wasted, you would take a much closer look. Imagine you really got into the numbers and found that instead of $400,000, the estimate was closer to $375,000. Would you be perturbed? Not likely. You still would have been made aware of a nearly $400,000 problem, and you would have been able to fix it. That is what you are doing with whiteboard economics—getting to know how hard and close of a look a problem or opportunity deserves. If it is potentially big, there will be plenty of time to get some help along the way from people whose job it is to get all the precise numbers and make sure they jive. For now, you do some quick math.

> When doing whiteboard economics, use words and phrases like *ballpark, rough estimate, more or less, best guess,* and *finger to the wind.*

You'll want to know if the problem involves tens of thousands, hundreds of thousands, millions, tens of millions, hundreds of millions—what's the order of magnitude? The size of the solution should be at least somewhat commensurate with the size of the problem you want to solve or the opportunity you want to seize. Do your best to turn all nonfinancial figures into money. Don't stop with percentages or ratios just because they are numbers. Your goal, because you are trying to build a business case, is to convert them to their cash equivalents. If you miss the conversion, you may also miss:

- Knowing the financial impact of solving the problem or seizing the opportunity
- Funding the right solutions, while inferior return-on-investment (ROI) solutions get money
- Securing proper ROI which remains elusive and hidden
- Having a solid business case to compare alternative solutions against

- Moving people toward consensus based on agreement on an objective rationale

Could versus Should

When you convert hard evidence into impact, it answers the questions: "How big is the impact if you decide to do something about it?" and "What is it costing you by not solving the problem?" If the problem is never fixed (worst-case scenario), then what happens? If you never adopt this strategy, what are the implications? If everything goes right (best-case scenario), what do you gain? It is the justification that proves you *should* act. Of all the things you *could* do, this better be something you *should* pay attention (time, people, and money) to. If the payoff doesn't justify the attention, don't do it! If the payoff is equivalent to little tremors people barely notice and nobody cares about, don't bother. You are after the impact, short- and long-term, direct and opportunity, tangible and intangible. That's why you hardwire the measurable alert into your nervous system. When you actually have evidence (hard or soft), convert the evidence into impact.

 Rule 5: Calculate the Impact. Convert hard evidence into impact; a move from the *could* to the *should* that shows the basic economic return.

The Five Golden Questions

With the measurable alert hardwired into your nervous system, be on the lookout for hard evidence. When you hear or offer something you can measure that is directly related to what you want to prevent or invent, your measurable alert should go off, and you can ask these five important questions (or whatever will accomplish the same outcome) that will convert hard evidence into impact:

1. How do you measure it?
2. What is it now?
3. What would you like it to be?
4. What's the value of the difference?
5. What's the value of the difference over time (months, years—the appropriate management horizon)?

For example, imagine you are a director in a travel services company. During a strategy meeting, one of your colleagues from client services brings an idea to the table.

Colleague: Moving our travel services online would make it easier for our customers to purchase by giving them better, faster access and would increase our market share.

businessThink: *How do you measure* market share for this particular product?

Colleague: Percent of market ownership for corporate travel clients.

businessThink: *What is it now?*

Colleague: Roughly 8 percent.

businessThink: *What would you like it to be* once you've given them better, quicker access online?

Colleague: Twelve percent.

businessThink: So what does each 1 percent market share equate to in financial terms?

Colleague: About $3 million in revenue, give or take 5 percent.

businessThink: So if you want to move from 8 to 12 percent, you're talking about an $8- to $12-million opportunity?

Colleague: Yeah, roughly.

businessThink: Okay. So, since our strategic plan covers the next three to five years, are we realistically looking at a $36- to $48-million opportunity by doing this?

Colleague: We hadn't run those numbers yet, but I would be surprised if marketing and IT couldn't get behind that figure.

This example is simplistic, but you get the idea. And when the value of the difference is immediately apparent in money, you can drop the question, "What's the value of the difference?" For example, one of your colleagues from sales makes an observation:

Colleague: Not having account-management software is hurting sales.

businessThink: What are sales now?

Colleague: $500 million.

businessThink: Let's say we had account-management software that was really doing the job. What would we expect sales to be then?

Colleague: $550 million.

businessThink: So over the next three to five years you'd be looking at revenue growth of $150 million to $250 million?

The real art form is in quantifying the impact when the value of the difference is not immediately apparent in dollars. This will require you to ask a few more questions that may not be as apparent and easy. For instance, if someone believes the key issue is quality:

businessThink: How do you measure quality?

Colleague: Number of rejections per thousand units.

businessThink: What is the current rejection rate?

Colleague: Ten per thousand units.

businessThink: Let's say we were successful with this TQM project. What would you expect it to be?

Colleague: Five per thousand units.

businessThink: What's the value of the difference?

Colleague: Well, big bucks!

And that's the problem. You have just asked the other person to do a lot of math in their head. And they may not be able to. Chunk it down and take it one step at a time—together.

You and Your Calculator Can Take a Flying . . .

If you want your colleagues to feel involved and have a sense of shared ownership in the impact or payoff, do some whiteboard math together to come up with the amount. Involve others, especially if they are from other functions or departments with different agendas and budgets. Don't sit there with your calculator and spend five minutes punching buttons and announce, "Wow, your department has a $3-million problem!" At that point, they don't have a $3-million problem, even if your numbers are right. You and your calculator have a $3-million problem! Work on the problem or opportunity *with* them, not *for* them. They need a sense of ownership from the beginning. Don't start excluding them when determining the impact.

If the numbers come up big, don't gloat, sneer, or point fingers. At this point it will serve you, and others, well if you fall on the conservative side with your estimate. It will be better if others considering your business case think you have been conservative rather than overreaching. So you might say something like, "That seems like a large number. Is that realistic? Is it possible we could be overstating the impact?"

This gives others a chance to modify it or come up with a number everyone believes in. Remember that the goal is not to get them, the goal is to get real with an accurate sense of how big the number really is. When they do come up with a number they feel better about, you can still ask, "As we share our business case with others in the organization, are they likely to start nodding their heads in agreement with those numbers, or are they likely to wonder what we were smoking when we came up with them?" If the numbers are still too high, modify them. If the impact still seems big enough, you should proceed; if it doesn't, it *may* be over. There is one other question you need to ask to see if it's really over. That is the point of the next chapter.

Voodoo Economics

To ease your mind a little more about the "science" of finance and economics, here is an example of hard-core financial analysis we learned from our combined years of business school and real-life school. When I (Dave) was working for a company as vice president of sales, they asked me to take on the role of chief operating officer. That meant I had to get good at numbers beyond sales forecasting, bonuses, and commissions. I wasn't that good with numbers, but I had a battery of people to help me make sense of it all. Here's what I learned about something that sounds big and bad called *discounted cash flow analysis.* Let's say you have three proposed ideas (projects, proposals, business plans—three of anything really), and you have to figure out which one you *should* do for the best return on investment—after all, that's what investors and shareholders want to hear about.

First, you project what you expect the revenues to be over 5, 10, and 15 years. How do you think people come up with these numbers? They might look at market expansion, historic revenue growth patterns, marketing spending levels, and anticipated increase in customer demand. Even with all that data, they still have to do the best they can to make an educated guess as to what is possible in the future. And it *is* a guess.

The next step is to project the costs out 5, 10, and 15 years into the future. Maybe you expect some process efficiencies, or there may be some potential increases in some costs, yada, yada. Again, it's a guess. So far, the numbers we have are really hard-core, precise numbers, right? (If you're wondering, the answer is *no.*) Next, you simply subtract the costs you projected from the revenue you projected, and you have a new number that may represent gross margins or profit. Then you multiply those profits by the average weighted cost of capital (which is another guess—nobody knows what that really is). So you have a stream of guesses about revenue, you subtract the stream of guesses about costs, and you divide that by a guess about the weighted cost of capital, and you come up with net present value. When you look at the numbers, what happens if you don't like what you see? You change your guesses and modify your assumptions! Often you can get them to be what you believe they should be.

And that's what many people call hard-core financial analysis. The only thing that makes this more rigorous than whiteboard economics is that they plug it into a spreadsheet. Oh, and someone with financial credentials rubs their eyebrows over the paper. Not exactly as intimidating as it seems, is it? Nobody is pretending these guesses are reality. As abnormal as it sounds, the exercise has a purpose: to take guesses and opinions about the future, and talk about them in the common denominator of money.

The businessThink Mirror

In the following test, read each statement and check the box that best describes you. Even though the statements are focused specifically on you, ask the same questions of your department, division, management or executive team, and company.

The businessThink Economics Test

	Yes	Sporadically	I'm in the red
1. I estimate the financial impact of not solving problems or creating new opportunities.	❑	❑	❑
2. I involve people in estimating the financial impact of problems or opportunities on the company.	❑	❑	❑
3. Once I've made a decision, I feel confident in presenting a strong business case for the recommendations.	❑	❑	❑
4. When calculating the impact of a business problem or opportunity, I consistently ask the five golden questions.	❑	❑	❑
5. When I make business decisions, the ROI to the business is clear to me, and to others who are making the decision or will be affected by it.	❑	❑	❑
6. I use financial data to help people move toward consensus based on a more objective rationale.	❑	❑	❑

RULE 6

Explore the Ripple Effect

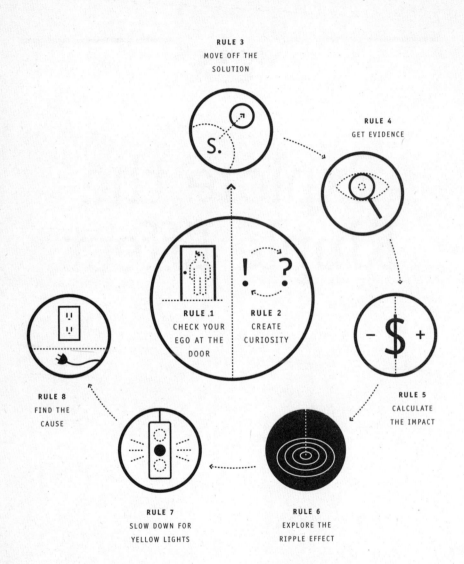

RULE 3
MOVE OFF THE
SOLUTION

RULE 4
GET EVIDENCE

RULE 1
CHECK YOUR
EGO AT THE
DOOR

RULE 2
CREATE
CURIOSITY

RULE 8
FIND THE
CAUSE

RULE 5
CALCULATE
THE IMPACT

RULE 7
SLOW DOWN FOR
YELLOW LIGHTS

RULE 6
EXPLORE THE
RIPPLE EFFECT

When exploring a problem or an opportunity, calculating the impact gives you a financial number to assess the value of a solution. However, the financial impact only represents the effect on one part of the company (yours). Even though it's important to you, it's only one piece of the puzzle. Rarely does a problem or opportunity only affect one person, department, or part of the company. Imagine throwing a rock into the middle of a pond: It makes a splash and sinks, and the ripples move farther and farther out. The same thing applies to most problems or opportunities in a company.

Something is going on somewhere inside the company; it's making a local splash, and then starts to ripple throughout the rest of the company. The impact or cost of the problem can *increase* based on who or what else in the company is affected. Or, it may *decrease* in importance when weighed against other priorities. It may be big for you (or your department), but when weighed against other priorities under the same scrutiny for *strategic fit* and financial return, it doesn't take precedence.

Every company has an explicit or implicit mission, values, and key strategies or initiatives that are imperative to the growth and survival of the company. To the degree that you understand how what you are trying to solve fits into the bigger picture, the eventual solution will help meet companywide goals, tie into objectives of other departments and people, and help generate results for the entire company—not just a functional few.

Exploring the Ripple Effect will give you the tools to widen your functional lens and capture the bigger picture and the broader impact of problems or opportunities on the company. It will also provide a way to make sure you know who or what else in the company is affected that moves beyond functional silos, cubicle walls, and organization chart structures.

CHAPTER THIRTEEN

Who and What Else Is Affected?

You, like every businessperson on the planet, are often limited by the functional dialect of your native tongue and your isolated role; separated by degrees, certificates, and cubicle walls. It is essential to consider who or what else is potentially affected by the issues at hand. Remember Paul Nutt's research:

> Only 7 percent of decisions (roughly 26 of 356) are made after considering long-term priorities or conferring with colleagues.[1]

functionThink

Take this example: Bright human resources people know their own stuff—recruiting, compensation, learning, culture, benefits, safety, labor law, talent, and the like. They're up on all the latest human resources thinking and innovations published by other well-known human resources people. Clearly, their approach to solutions will have a human resources bias. When you are focused solely on your craft, it's easy to lose sight of the bigger picture of the business.

> *Because you often think like those who*
> *surround you, and act on what you think,*
> *your group develops its own secret language*
> *that nobody else really understands,*
> *and your solutions are designed to meet*
> *your needs, and nobody else's.*

If you don't understand how others will define success, you may get the results you want, but not the results anyone else wants or needs. The functional assumption becomes that this is just a *group* issue, and nobody else is affected (which is wrong), or you may feel that you know better than others, and everyone will dig this—after all, what is good for human resources (or the favorite department of your choice—maybe yours) must be good for everybody.

 Rule 6: Explore the Ripple Effect. Who or what else in the company is affected by the current problem or the opportunity under consideration?

> The people who get sucked into isolated and exclusionary thinking lose sight of the big picture of the business as a whole, and instead of businessThink, they get *functionThink.*

businessThink is designed to overcome this functional tendency. It's not like people are trying consciously to hurt others or leave them out. The business lens functional people look through is focused, and while that focus picks up some cool images, it sometimes narrows their view and misses what's outside their functional frame. They need both the functional close-up lens *and* the wide-angle business lens. As businesspeople, don't mind your *own* business, mind *the* business. *functionThink* (managementThink, marketingThink, salesThink, humanresourceThink, r&dThink, financeThink), without the perspective of businessThink, isolates people, problems, opportunities, and eventually solutions. Sometimes, even with the best of intentions, people overgeneralize in promoting their functional view and become organizationally blind.

The functional blindness can lead to the following problems:

- Solutions that serve only a few local people and not the entire company

- Missing strategic fit of solutions into major company initiatives

- Confusion in weighing your priorities against other priorities going on in the company

- Missing the full scope of the impact

- "Solving" something that doesn't need to be solved (One group's gain may be another group's pain.)

Guilty until Proven Innocent

It is difficult, if not impossible, to have or build a killer solution if you've never talked to all the people who are currently being affected by the problem. The challenge, though, is that everyone is busy, and you struggle to determine who or what else would be affected, and the addiction to speed doesn't help. As a result, what seems like a good decision to move forward with a solution ultimately blows up. Because a lot of seemingly good decisions explode upon implementation, dysfunctional decision-making practices (multiple approvals, drawn-out decisions, layers of red tape) have arisen to combat the constant flow of dysfunctional projects and myopic solutions. Because of this long history of dysfunction, you are guilty until your businessThinking proves you innocent. The better you understand the ripple effect, the more likely it is you will have a solution that truly works for the whole company and is sustainable. Figure 13.1 shows a visual representation of the ripple effect.

Looking at the ripple effect, you need to know how it is linked to the mission, vision, and key strategies of the company. What is going on in the company that affects *every* decision made, not simply the one under consideration? We know this isn't something that has never occurred to you before. It's not rocket science. Yet, it continues to astound us, the number of people who fail to take time to understand the organizational context and culture of their own company, not to mention their primary customers or market. The ripple effect reminds you to consider what else is (or might be) going on in the company, and get whatever solution you land on to fit into that bigger picture.

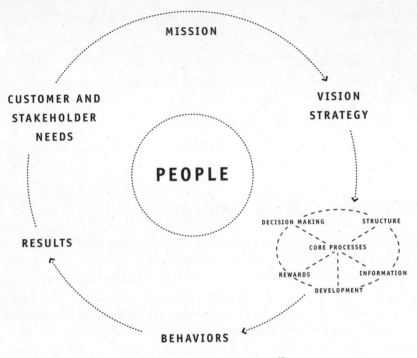

Figure 13.1   The ripple effect.

When the Impact Is Small

As you look at the ripple effect, at any point in your discussions, anyone might reach the conclusion that the impact of the problem is not substantial. The financial value may not be great relative to the company's overall priorities, or all that impressive relative to the size of other divisional or functional goals. On a closer look, maybe you would place your ideas on the lower end of a scale of 1 to 10. For whatever reason, if you sense that the opportunity either is not important or is not urgent, you have a couple of choices:

- Move on to something else.
- Consider the worst-case scenario if you do nothing.

It might sound something like this:

businessThink: If this problem is only costing us $100,000 a year, the problem may be cheaper than a solution. Let's say we did nothing and watched this over the next couple of years—would anyone even care? Could we live with that?

Or, if this is only a 5, doesn't it seem likely that we would be better off spending our money on strategies that are 8s, 9s, and 10s?

Asking any of these questions may seem counterintuitive. We say that after watching countless people make valiant attempts to convince others that the impact is much more important or urgent than they perceive it to be. If the project is an 8, 9, or 10 for you, but when exploring the ripple effect you determine it's a 5, 6, or 7 for the company as a whole, your best option might be to give up the time, people, and money for something better (a *should*).

When Giving Up the Solution Is "Wrong"

It might be that your colleagues are willing to give up on the pursuit of a solution, because they think the impact is small. But you see the impact as being greater than they do, and you think they are making a mistake. It's possible you may have expertise that they don't, and they don't know what they don't know. At this point, you have little to lose—if they don't change their perception of the impact, you won't be able to help them or the company with any solution. It is appropriate at this point to present the information you think they lack. Making a strong case might look like the following example.

Let's say you're consulting with the call-center operations in your company, and you uncover the fact that there is 40 percent turnover in one of the call centers. You also happen to know that the industry standard (evidence from the outside) is 20 percent. So, in making your case, you businessThink:

businessThink: I read that turnover for call-center employees in our industry is roughly 20 percent annually. We are currently at 40 percent. If the industry standard really is 20 percent, what is the impact of having 20 percent more turnover than our competition?

Colleague: I don't think it's that big of a deal. People who have been around for a long time become both cynical and more expensive. New people are cheaper and more enthusiastic. We actually like the 40 percent turnover.

businessThink: Well, you might be right. Do you mind if I ask you a few questions based on my experience?

You might then ask them how they feel about some of the following issues, or you could provide them with data about the true cost of turnover.

- *Reputation.*   Because of a bad corporate reputation for losing so many people, is it harder to hire quality people?

- *Lower customer satisfaction.*   Is the customer tired of dealing with someone new who doesn't know the return policies?

- *Paperwork.*   What's the cost to move people in and out of the company?

- *Training costs.*   Is there enough time for new people to catch up, and understand our products and services to generate sales?

- *Lost productivity.*   Are there fewer experienced workers? Is there a less flexible workforce? Is there a loss of production because of that?

- *Increased hiring costs.*   What are the costs for hiring agencies and company time?

- *Unemployment taxes.*   Are we paying higher unemployment taxes because of our turnover?

- *Cost of temporary help.*   Are we paying more to hire temps because of being short of help?

- *Error rate.*   Are we experiencing more errors because of inexperienced or disgruntled workers?

In sharing your technical brilliance with others, just because you strongly, fervently, passionately believe you are right, doesn't mean you are. Increasing your conviction doesn't make you more right. Piling on with more data may not persuade anyone. It rarely does. Try not to confuse certainty with reality.

People could change their perception because of the questions you ask, and how you ask them. You may have an opportunity to help the company get a solution it really needs, not to mention the other departments that could benefit from your thinking. Or they won't change their perception, and you can move on. Functional expertise is vital, and with businessThink added to it, it becomes much more powerful and persuasive.

With that in mind, feel free to advocate what you perceive to be true, knowing that your perception is only that—*your* perception.

Now that you have moved off the solution to the relevant, underlying business issues, have evidence and impact for the most important issues, and know the ripple effect of the problem or opportunity, you now take a close look at the constraints on or potential roadblocks to doing something about it. After all, if the issues are compelling, and the evidence and impact are solid, why hasn't the company done something about it before now? If it's simply gone unnoticed, what could stop you from being successful?

The businessThink Mirror

In the following test, read each statement and check the box that best describes you. Even though the statements are focused specifically on you, ask the same questions of your department, division, management or executive team, and company.

The businessThink Ripple Effect Test

	No problem	Now and again	function-Think
1. I know what role my group plays in the overall strategies and objectives of the company.	❏	❏	❏
2. I think beyond the immediate impact of proposed ideas or solutions by exploring who or what else in the company would be affected.	❏	❏	❏
3. In order to get an accurate and complete picture of the financial impact on the company, I use knowledge about our business (e.g., marketplace trends, clients, industry, services, challenges).	❏	❏	❏
4. Before moving forward on a functional solution, I weigh it against other priorities and initiatives going on in the company.	❏	❏	❏
5. I meet periodically with key people to maintain my awareness about top business strategies and initiatives.	❏	❏	❏
6. I help address issues arising from people who may be negatively impacted by the matter at hand.	❏	❏	❏
7. When considering a possible solution, I explore what has prevented a successful solution in the past, or what might prevent one in the future.	❏	❏	❏

Slow Down for
Yellow Lights

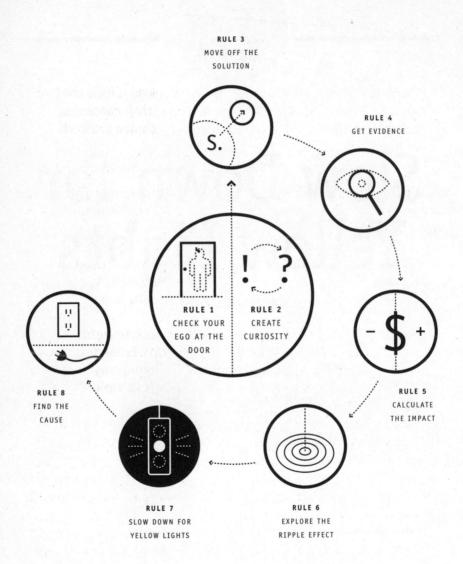

RULE 3
MOVE OFF THE
SOLUTION

RULE 4
GET EVIDENCE

S.

RULE 1
CHECK YOUR
EGO AT THE
DOOR

RULE 2
CREATE
CURIOSITY

RULE 5
CALCULATE
THE IMPACT

RULE 8
FIND THE
CAUSE

RULE 7
SLOW DOWN FOR
YELLOW LIGHTS

RULE 6
EXPLORE THE
RIPPLE EFFECT

> **People may clutch to the hope that if their thinking is lucid and logical, their language is persuasive and clear, and their conclusions are concrete, then the solution will be readily adopted and work. Not necessarily.**

When you are considering the scope of a problem or the size of an opportunity, don't pretend that if you *could* craft a solution, you would somehow arrive in Happy Valley and would coast merrily down the path to success. Look ahead to what could go wrong. What (or even who) might be out to get you? You'll need to look at any possible solution with your eyes wide open. What could sidetrack your efforts or shut any solution down?

> *The essence of slowing down for yellow lights is asking the hard question, "If this is such a big deal, what has stopped the company from doing something about it before now?"*

Often, when you're this close to having what you need to justify a solution, this question doesn't even occur to you; the addiction to speed begins to resurface. You start to realize you are close to making the pain of some problem go away, or you imagine the payoff of a new opportunity. Either way, you want to rush toward the excitement of building a solution.

If the question does occur to you, you're often hesitant to ask it, because you're afraid of what the answer might be. Or you're afraid that it might prove to be a political land mine or a career-limiting (possibly career-ending) inquiry. However, not asking the question may produce those same results. For the sake of everyone involved, you'll need to muster the courage to ask the hard question—just ask it in a soft way. When you slow down long enough to consider what has, will, or could stop any solution from working, you'll potentially save yourself a lot of wasted energy and improve the likelihood of success for the solution, and you may save the company valuable, scarce resources.

Slowing Down for Yellow Lights will give you the tools to be on the alert for anything that could stop a solution dead in its tracks. Two vital questions you will ask are: "What has stopped us from successfully doing something about this before now?" and "What might stop us in the future?"

CHAPTER FOURTEEN

Let's Get Real— or Let's Not Play

When you are driving, especially when you are anxious to arrive somewhere important, and you approach a yellow light, what do you do? If you are like most people, you gun it to beat the light. A yellow light has become the universal symbol for *speed up!* Unfortunately, many people use that same response in business. They hear something that concerns them, see a reaction that could spell trouble, feel they are running into a snag, and they speed up to avoid running into their own worst fears. When they think they see a big potential return-on-investment (ROI) sign ahead, they're tempted to put the pedal to the metal.

Ultimately, they are afraid the light will turn red. Experience in business has convinced people that hitting a red light is failure, and so when they see yellow, they close their eyes and speed up, hoping they make it through.

> If you can't slow down for yellow lights to businessThink, it's hard to get real—either with yourself, with others, or about the solution the business needs.

businessThink requires that you deal with what's real. If hitting a red light is unavoidable, hit it as soon as possible—the sooner the better. Intellectually, people know that; emotionally, they resist it.

 Rule 7: Slow Down for Yellow Lights. If the problem or opportunity is so big, what has stopped us in the past from doing something about it, and what could stop us in the future?

Here are three ideas that allow you to manage yellow lights effectively:

- *Red lights are not failure.* Failure is making a red light needlessly more expensive (spending a lot more time, money, and company resources to hit the same red light that could have been reached very early in the game).

- *When you encounter a yellow light, slow down.* If you see it, hear it, or feel it, find a way to say it—tactfully.

- *Turn the yellow lights to red or green.* Often, another person's criteria for resolution are less stringent than your own. If *they* turn the light to green, they're far more convinced than if you convince them.

During conversations, people will give you signals about how they are feeling and what they are thinking. That's where your innate and hopefully well-tuned XQ kicks in. Those signals will come verbally (what they say to you), vocally (how they say it— their inflection, emphasis, tone, and pace), and visually (their nonverbal communication). You'll need acute awareness to sense all the signals. People will give you signals that will tell you the conversation has hit a yellow light. Remember the rule for yellow lights: *If you see it, hear it, or feel it, find a way to say it—tactfully.*

Slowing down relies on your awareness of what is going on and your choices of what to do about it (not to mention checking your ego). One very powerful choice is to state the obvious, hopefully without unneeded emotional charge. Here is a three-part response that seems to work well:

1. "I have a concern." (Or, "I am confused." Or, "I think we may have a problem.")

2. State the concern (or the confusion, or the potential problem).

3. Ask what they think should be done to resolve the yellow light. Listen until they feel you understand their point of

view. (Remember, you want them to solve it so they are convinced.)

State the Obvious

Here are examples of yellow lights and how you can effectively slow down for them.

Yellow Light: A committee may have already decided to allocate resources to something else.
businessThink:

1. I'm getting a feeling I'd like to run by you.

2. I sense that no matter how good my idea is, or even if the business case produces better ROI, the decision has already been made to do something else.

3. Am I off base?

Yellow Light: People seem unwilling to make a financial commitment.
businessThink:

1. I'm confused.

2. We said this project could save us tens of millions, yet you are only willing to invest tens of thousands.

3. What part of the *I* in ROI am I missing?

When you ignore yellow lights, they do exactly what yellow traffic lights do: They turn red, and you are stopped. If you run them, there are all kinds of accidents and risks waiting to happen. Let's get real—or let's not play. Ignoring yellow lights is a form of guessing, and you have committed to *no guessing.*

Red lights are not bad. They are just red lights. They don't mean you've missed an opportunity. They do mean you have hit an obstacle, which, if unresolved, *will* mean it's over. At least you are aware of what's going on and can do something about it.

Remember that a red light is not failure.
If you get a yellow light early and take your
best shot at resolving it, but can't, you have
saved a lot of valuable time and money. Failure is
making red lights needlessly more expensive.

Damn the Yellow Lights, Full Speed Ahead

Here is an example, with me (Mahan) as the goat. Once when I was in sales, I was calling on a large financial services firm. Because their offices were just a few blocks from another major client of mine, I invited an important partner from a large consulting firm to accompany me—so I could show off my tremendous talents. That was the first yellow light—I most definitely did not check my ego at the door. We were supposed to meet with the person championing our cause, the chief executive officer, and a vice president of marketing. When we arrived, we were informed my champion wasn't going to be there. He was flying in from out of town. That was the second yellow light, but I moved right ahead. As we were escorted up to the offices, we were informed that the CEO also couldn't make the meeting (another *major* yellow light). If I hadn't invited the VIP to accompany me, I might have called off the meeting. I still should have called it off—and didn't.

We then proceeded to meet with the vice president of marketing. At this point I was very angry and upset, and knew I was talking to the wrong person. I proceeded anyway (my ego would not be checked at any door known to mere mortals). I did my best to focus on the issues at hand. The vice president was very polite and answered all of my questions, yet every neuron in my body was screaming, "This is going nowhere!" It was a scene resplendent with yellow lights, multiple and flashing.

Had I had my wits about me instead of my ego, I would have said something like, "John, you are being very polite and courteous, and yet my intuition is telling me that this is going nowhere, and as soon as I walk out the door, nothing of substance will occur. What are you feeling at this point?" However, on this occasion, I lacked both the clarity and the courage. I said nothing, and sure enough, nothing happened. I wasn't fearless and flexible, and I didn't have fun.

It turned out that the vice president had selected another firm in advance, had committed to them, and had done everything in his power to make sure I didn't talk to the CEO or anyone else. In retrospect, the competitor's solution did not meet the company's needs—it failed miserably, and the vice president was let go. Small solace to my inability to practice what I teach, and what I usually do. Even if I had slowed down for the yellow lights, there was no guarantee I could have turned them to green. However, at least I could have been "real," or authentic. I would have had a chance to deal with what was really going on. The move to green or red could have been conscious and participatory rather than passive. Ahhh—continuous learning!

If This Is Such a Big Deal . . . ?

If you arrive at the conclusion that the impact of a problem or opportunity is big, a significant question should arise: "What has stopped you (or the company as a whole) from successfully resolving these issues before now?"

It's a yellow light, and you need to check it out. If this is a new opportunity with no history, the yellow-light question is "What, if anything, might prevent the successful implementation of this solution from going forward?"

The answer to this question can provide valuable insight. For whatever reason, it is often not asked. Perhaps you fear, at some level, that you really will hit something unsolvable and all your hard work and businessThinking will get shut down. Believe us, the odds of getting shut down are much greater if you don't ask (and get answers to) those questions.

Yellow lights can reveal obstacles or barriers from the past that no longer exist. That's good! You didn't have a budget before, and now you do. You didn't have various approvals, and now you do. It wasn't a top priority, and now it is. Or they have stopped us in the past, and nothing has changed. For instance:

- We haven't been able to get this adequately budgeted.
- We can't get buy-in from the executive committee.
- The XYZ group has a vested interest in killing it.
- Politics has always gotten in the way.
- It's been too complicated.
- We've had higher priorities.

If so, you know two things: The impact is big, and there is something real in front of you that can stop you from getting the impact you want. The question you ask is "What's different this time?" If nothing *is* different, it's likely nothing will *be* different. It is crucial to understand what blocked the solution in the past that might block it again. Hitting one of these roadblocks is a yellow light. You can say something like this:

businessThink: I have a concern. It sounds like even if we come up with the best possible solution, even if it really gets the results we discussed, it won't be adopted. Politics has killed it in the past and it will this time too. What do you think we should do?

You know the impact is big, and you won't make the best business decision possible unless the constraints are removed. If the constraints can't be removed, can they be managed or circumvented? If not, do you even want to proceed? *No!* The reason is vulnerability: Your solution won't be adopted, and even if it is adopted, the implementation of the solution may suffer.

Once again, you slow down for yellow lights by stating the obvious with tact and grace. Once you've removed any roadblocks and dealt with the yellow lights, and you're convinced that something is worth solving, the time has arrived to move to the next chapter and find out what is causing the problem in the first place.

The businessThink Mirror

In the following test, read each statement and check the box that best describes you. Even though the statements are focused specifically on you, ask the same questions of your department, division, management or executive team, and company.

The businessThink Yellow Lights Test

	Yes	Once in a while	Get-real time
1. If I hear, see, or sense something thatdoesn't make sense, I find a tactful way to state the obvious.	❏	❏	❏
2. If I find a solution that seems to make sense, and the problem seems to be high priority, I slow down to make sure we answer the question, "If this is so important, what has stopped us from successfully addressing this issue before now?"	❏	❏	❏
3. I look ahead to see what constraints might prevent us from achieving something that makes good business sense.	❏	❏	❏
4. I am willing to slow down and ask questions about topics that seem confusing or not obvious to people.	❏	❏	❏

Find the Cause

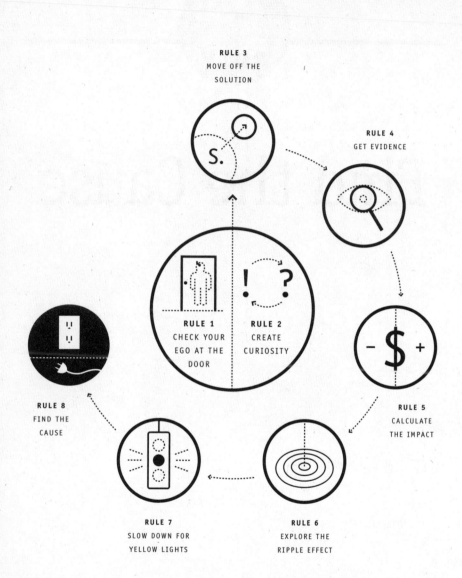

RULE 3
MOVE OFF THE SOLUTION

RULE 4
GET EVIDENCE

RULE 1
CHECK YOUR EGO AT THE DOOR

RULE 2
CREATE CURIOSITY

RULE 5
CALCULATE THE IMPACT

RULE 8
FIND THE CAUSE

RULE 7
SLOW DOWN FOR YELLOW LIGHTS

RULE 6
EXPLORE THE RIPPLE EFFECT

Up to this point in businessThinking, you have the evidence and impact to justify that something is a *should,* you know who or what else is affected, and the yellow lights have turned to green. You can confidently answer the questions "Where does it hurt and how bad?" or "How big is the opportunity, and what's the payoff?" Even though you have a compelling case that something needs to be done, you are not *quite* ready to solve the problem or capitalize on the opportunity. Having proof you *need* a solution (the effects), and knowing *what* solution you need are two different things.

> Unless you ask *why,* an attempt to solve a problem is like taking painkillers to cure a disease. You know the effects of the disease and the impact of the disease on the body, but you don't know what's causing the disease or where it is, and so the drug only masks the pain while the condition lives on, and worsens.

You may pick a completely different solution depending on *where* a solution needs to be applied, or whether you are treating symptoms or fixing the causes.

> *What kind of doctor would you be if your patient was bleeding faster and faster, and your only response was to increase the speed of the transfusion?*
> —Jeffrey Pfeffer, Thomas D. Dee Professor of Organizational Behavior, Stanford Graduate School of Business[1]

Finding the Cause will give you the tools to dig for the underlying reason for the symptoms, and make sure you're treating the cause of the problem rather than the effects.

CHAPTER FIFTEEN

Why Ask Why?

Not long ago, my wife and I (Steve) purchased a new home, our first home. We loved it. It had everything that was important to us: a beautiful view, plenty of sunlight, a safe neighborhood, and good schools nearby. After about two years in our "wonderful" new home, we noticed some cracks in the foundation walls and basement floor. We didn't know if it was something to be concerned about or not. We'd heard that every home settles a bit, and that small cracks in the concrete foundation were normal. As first-time homebuyers, how would we know? Without any expertise, I made a quick trip to the local do-it-yourself home-warehouse store, purchased some concrete patching material, went home, slapped it over the cracks, and prayed.

Finally, a friend who actually knew something and had more experience than we did told us our problem was not normal. Soon we noticed more serious things: doors not shutting, cracks in the upstairs walls, leaking windows, loud pops from the house settling, the deck floor sinking—to name only a few. Everything in our house was slowly becoming "indoor-outdoor." Meanwhile, the impact started to sink in: Our lives were being disrupted, our home had lost all market value and had become unsellable—we couldn't move if we needed to—and the potential financial result could bankrupt us. We had enough evidence to cause real concern, and the magnitude of the impact forced us to become intensely interested in the *why*. We called an expert (often important when digging for the *why*) and kept asking why through research, testing, and the collection of evidence.

After asking enough whys, we discovered that the house was built on an old ravine filled with scrap-ridden, uncompacted dirt. Lucky us! That was the *cause* of the house's taking its own personal journey toward the center of the earth—the *why*. Evidence, like the growing sunroof in our son's bedroom, told us something bad was happening (the effects), impact motivated us to move with urgency, and asking why eventually told us what was causing the bad stuff to happen. If we hadn't done a little more research to find the *cause,* it would have been major-league guessing to figure out what to fix or who to sue—uh, er, *involve*—based solely on the effects. When it's a *physical* thing like fixing a house, the *why* or cause is not usually too hard to find. Expensive, yes, but hard, no.

> **For every thousand hacking at the leaves of evil there is one hacking at the root.**
>
> **–HENRY DAVID THOREAU**

The refined art form is finding the *why* when it isn't exactly a physical thing like a sinking house. The real-life laboratory of business involves intelligent, experienced people and constantly shifting priorities and organizational contexts—not to mention the addiction to speed we all give in to now and then. It's not exactly like chemistry, where you merely plug in some formulas and see what reaction you get. This complexity is the reason we suggest you spend the time digging for *why* only after you have the evidence and impact to prove that it's worth a solution.

If you miss the *why,* you may also:

- Select and apply the wrong solution
- Cause other problems
- Create expectations that the problem will go away, and then it doesn't
- Waste the investment of time, people, and money that the real solution needs

The *Why* Posse

Simply knowing you need to ask the question "Why?" doesn't make it easy. Intellectually, it seems simple and straightforward, but in real-time application, it's often emotionally or psychologically hard to commit to and follow through on. When you dig for the *why,* you are asking people to share their beliefs, opinions, observations, or viewpoints. They may share information based on data. They may have customer input. They may have research. They may have surveys. They may have nothing more than an opinion. Sometimes flawed thinking is exposed.

Because asking why often penetrates to the heart of an issue, it can be perceived as the work of a posse in search of the guilty party, and the "wanted" don't intend to get lynched.

People with ego assume that they already know the answer—so why waste more time on it? They don't want to be questioned about their thinking. They may feel their intelligence is being insulted, or that they're not competent to make the decision. Since the pursuit of *why* can make people feel defensive (and therefore make you look offensive), you'll need to check your ego and have the right intent to create an honest, open environment that will elicit the vital information without making people feel they are being hunted down and attacked.

Your intent is not to hunt down the guilty, but to invest the time it takes to understand *why* something is happening: What's the cause? You have the responsibility to make it comfortable and helpful to ask the question "Why?" Without it, the solution won't address the underlying cause.

Disclaimer

The intent of this chapter is to make sure readers are aware of and understand the need to find out why *before* they start putting solutions into place. This chapter is not a complete, comprehensive dissertation on root-cause analysis. There are big, fat books you can read, and college degrees you can get in that stuff. Or, you can go get an expert who knows how to read the fine print when it comes to root-cause analysis. With what you already know from the tools of businessThink, you can begin a lot of it yourself.

Why? Why? Why? Why? Why?

Here's a story we've heard many times in many places and settings that illustrates the power of digging for the *why*. Years ago, at the Jefferson Memorial in Washington, D.C., the U.S. Department of Parks and Recreation had a problem. The stones of the Jefferson Memorial were deteriorating badly, and it was giving the maintenance people fits. Meanwhile, tourists were complaining that the memorial was in disrepair or was being neglected. Here is the original list of issues:

- Memorial stone is deteriorating.
- Tourists are complaining.
- Maintenance workers are spending too much time cleaning.
- Image of the monument is not up to standards.
- Costs are up for cleaning supplies and materials.

Imagine you're the director. The solution might seem obvious: Replace the stones. After all, the monument was built in 1943, and it's about time to refurbish the old memorial. But when you ask why the stones are deteriorating, you discover that it's probably because the grounds crew has to clean the stones more frequently than normal. Once you find out that the grounds crew is cleaning the stones all the time, there are a number of possible solutions you could apply to the problem:

- Use less-abrasive cleanser.
- Use less-harsh cleaning chemicals.
- Replace the stones so less cleaning is needed.
- Live with it and explain to the tourists that it's just an old building.

But you have other monuments with the same stone, and those monuments aren't deteriorating or in need of constant cleaning, so you ask, "*Why* are we cleaning the Jefferson Memorial all the time?"

The answer? The pigeons who frequently visit the stones on the memorial are leaving too many calling cards. Ahh—just eliminate the pigeons, right?

Or, you ask, "*Why* all the pigeons?"

They feed on the heavy spider population.

This is where you might be tempted to implement a solution. You might be asking yourself, "Why am I paying these people? Can't they just solve the problem?" It might seem you've hit the "duh" factor—buy some bug spray, and get rid of the spiders. If you get rid of the spiders, you get rid of the birds; and if the birds are gone, the droppings are gone; and if the droppings are gone, no more frequent cleanings; and voila, the problem is solved. The solution would be fast, immediate—and temporary and premature.

Why are there so many spiders?

The spiders are attracted by the huge moth population.

Again, a number of solutions seem obvious. Insecticide could wipe out the moths *and* the spiders. The downside to this solution is that maybe the chemicals could also damage the stones even more. And besides, who wants the smell of chemicals? Couldn't that affect the tourists and the maintenance workers who visit frequently? It would be easy to say, "We'll just have to live with those downsides." The question is, if you get rid of all the insects, the problem is solved, right? *Wrong! Why* all the moths?

The moths are attracted by the monument's lights during their twilight swarming period.

At this point you've discovered the cause. Why are the moths attracted to the lights? Who knows? It's in their DNA. You just know they *are* attracted to the lights, and that's causing a chain reaction of events. Once you've hit the *why* mother lode, think about the solution options and play them out.

So what's the solution? Turn on the lights two hours later. Get rid of the early lights, and you get rid of most of the moths; no moths, no spiders; get rid of the spiders, and you say goodbye to the pigeons; eliminate the pigeons, and you save the stones from becoming the pigeons' personal rest room. Not only that, you save money on the light bill, and all the premature solutions (and their costs in time and money) have been avoided and haven't caused other problems. Asking why took time, but the solution you've chosen has a better likelihood of addressing the causes. Had any other solution along the way been chosen, it wouldn't have fixed anything—just masked it and created other problems that would require time and money to solve.

From the *What* and *How* to the *Why*

In the Jefferson Memorial case, they had evidence. They knew the impact. They had enough reason to find a solution. Without the *why*, the solution would have been premature and could have caused more problems. For purposes of readability, we have condensed the process to make it easy to follow. When you business-Think (move off the solution, get the evidence, calculate the impact, etc.), if you want to get started on finding the cause, here's how you move to the *why*:

1. *When you originally moved off the solution, you made a list of issues.* Take the highest-priority item from that list of issues, and ask why that particular thing is happening. In the example, imagine that the most important issue on the list was "The stones on the monument are deteriorating." Make a *why* list of *all* the things that could *contribute to* or *cause* the stones' deterioration.

2. *Now take the most important cause from the list you've just created.* Make another list of all the *whys* for that particular issue.

3. *Keep going until you hit the most important* why *on your list of issues.* In our experience, it usually takes three to five times of asking why to identify the cause.

You'll need the persistence to keep asking why with the right intent until you are confident you have identified the real cause. Your search for the *why* must be preceded by something that's justified by businessThinking. Once you've identified the real cause, you have to start formulating a solution, and you'll have options. Regardless of which option you choose, you'll have to find the time, people, and money that will be required to make the solution happen successfully. That's where we're headed in the next chapter.

The businessThink Mirror

In the following test, read each statement and check the box that best describes you. Even though the statements are focused specifically on you, ask the same questions of your department, division, management or executive team, and company.

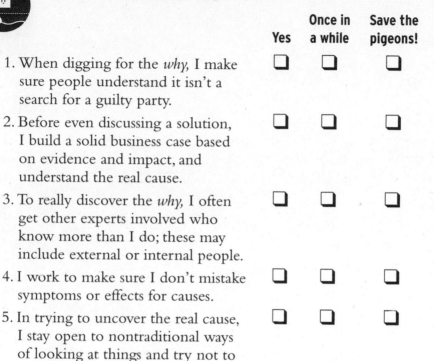

The businessThink Why? Test

	Yes	Once in a while	Save the pigeons!
1. When digging for the *why,* I make sure people understand it isn't a search for a guilty party.	❑	❑	❑
2. Before even discussing a solution, I build a solid business case based on evidence and impact, and understand the real cause.	❑	❑	❑
3. To really discover the *why,* I often get other experts involved who know more than I do; these may include external or internal people.	❑	❑	❑
4. I work to make sure I don't mistake symptoms or effects for causes.	❑	❑	❑
5. In trying to uncover the real cause, I stay open to nontraditional ways of looking at things and try not to "peek at the answers" before I understand the question.	❑	❑	❑

Note: If you would like to measure the businessThink readiness of a decision, idea, or strategy you're thinking about implementing, or would like to use a free "quickthink" tool to evaluate the business strength of something already in place, please visit **www. businessthink.biz/quickthink**.

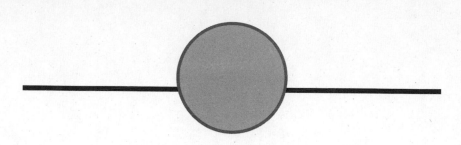

The Last Mile

CHAPTER SIXTEEN

Pay Attention: Time, People, and Money

Let's review where you are in businessThinking. At this point you've applied the following rules:

Rule 1: Check Your Ego at the Door. You've checked your ego, maybe several times, and worked delicately with the egos of others to keep dialogue open.

Rule 2: Create Curiosity. You've entered discussions with a healthy energy for asking questions, and have temporarily set aside your own knowledge and expertise as you have gathered other perspectives from your company's collective intellectual diversity.

Rule 3: Move Off the Solution. Rather than prematurely focusing on the solution itself, you've moved off the solution to get to the underlying business issues, carefully making sure you're not guessing, and focused your attention on the vital few issues.

Rule 4: Get Evidence. You've gathered proof that the business problem or opportunity exists by collecting soft evidence, and

then turned soft evidence into hard evidence that the business can measure.

 Rule 5: Calculate the Impact. In order to determine that this is a *should* and not a *could,* you've converted hard evidence into a financial equivalent to make sure that there is a worthwhile impact or payoff.

 Rule 6: Explore the Ripple Effect. You've carefully considered who or what else in the company is affected by the problem or opportunity. You've also considered the relative weight of the importance of this issue compared to other initiatives in the company.

 Rule 7: Slow Down for Yellow Lights. You know what has stopped the company from successfully doing something about this before now, or what might stop you in the future.

 Rule 8: Find the Cause. You've identified the cause producing the symptoms that are showing up, and you're convinced the solution will treat the cause of the problem rather than just the effects.

You now have a compelling business case, or you would have stopped long ago. All the yellow lights have turned to green, and you're ready to talk about the investment required for the solution. If you're not the only one deciding, you'll be presenting your case to others involved in making a decision. Even though you have a business case that would blow Jack Welch away, if you stop here you'll have wasted the entire effort. People can talk all they want in business about how much they like your ideas and proposed solutions, but until they pay attention, it's only talk. The corporate version of paying attention is when they allocate time, people, and money. If you stop now, there are some serious downsides. Here is an example:

The Best Idea Wins—or Not!

We know the team members who worked on a project researching a new product offering. They had done in-depth research, identified the market size, gathered demographics, and analyzed and compared the competitors' products, and they had a compelling business case to move forward. These guys were business-

Thinkers extraordinaire. They worked hard to arrange a meeting with the CEO, a division president, and an executive vice president. When they made their presentation, they demonstrated that the new offering, though yet to be created, delivered what the executives wanted. At the end of the meeting, they asked each executive, "On a scale of 1 to 10, how do you personally feel about this opportunity?"

Enthusiastically, each one gave it a 10. The CEO added that the company should bolt it on as a major plank of the company's strategy. Victory was assured immediately following the meeting, when the team was given a trophy that said, "The Best Idea Wins!" The celebrations were euphoric—and turned out to be premature.

Even though they made a strong business case, they forgot one small thing: They never asked the company to pay attention by allocating time, people, and money. They expected that funding and staffing would automatically follow, but it didn't happen. Instead, phone calls went unreturned, and the opportunity started to fade away. It took months to recover and rework their plan to get the project moving forward again. They felt first-hand the pain of guessing about three small but powerful questions.

If you don't ask about the *timing,* getting the right *people,* and the cold, hard *cash,* you are at risk. At this stage in the game, you only need to do a quick check as you ask about the resources you think will be needed; stay at a high level. Even though you have a lot of good information, and you're starting to get a sense of what the solution options are, you haven't singled out any particular solution. You don't have a detailed timeline, no Gantt charts, no vendors waiting at the door, or any specifics on the solution; you may be on your way—you're just not there yet. However, even if you've discovered what you think is a *should* for the business, you can't proceed (or succeed) if others don't agree it's worth paying attention to. This chapter includes some language examples you can use to see if the company is willing to ante up.

Find the Time

The first resource you need to get clear on is *time*—when do you want to start the project, and when would you like to see the results in place? If you want to start immediately and finish in a short time frame, you will need more people. If you can take longer to finish, you may need fewer people. Because the timing of the project affects the number of people needed, and that, in turn, will affect how much money you need, start with the timing questions. The questions about timing are pretty straightforward:

- When are you hoping to get started on this project?
- When do you want to have the results of the project in place?

Timing isn't a tough or delicate subject to talk about—you just have to remember to ask about it. However, if you skip it, it causes misunderstanding, frustrates people, and slows down the process of getting a decision made. The goal here is to make sure you and your colleagues are on the same page.

Sometimes the people you're selling the idea to have unrealistic expectations about time. Sometimes people want it too soon, especially if they are addicted to speed. If they're in

MORE

FASTER

PANIC

mode, find out what's driving the urgency. Maybe the need for speed is real and justified, and maybe it's not. Sometimes you bump into the exact opposite—people suffer from analysis paralysis, and don't want to rush into anything for fear of breaking any land speed records. Since the concerns are predictable, you can have some predictable, effective responses. For example, if someone wants the solution yesterday (or too soon), you might say something like this:

businessThink: I have a concern. I think it's possible to get the results we talked about. I don't think it's possible to get started that soon. What do you think we should do? If we were all completely convinced we could get the results, and it would take two months instead of three weeks, could we still move forward?

On the other hand, you might have someone who suggests a starting date for an important project that is six months to a year down the road.

businessThink: I'm confused. We agreed that this is costing us
$10 million a year, and you don't want to get started until the
middle of next fiscal year. By then this problem will cost us an
additional $7 million. What am I missing?

You can say something like that only if you've done a good job
businessThinking; otherwise, you won't have the business case to
challenge the suggested delay. If in fact they are serious about
delaying the start of building a solution, there are at least three concerns that may come to mind:

- Do other people who have a say in this really see this as a priority? Not having been in on the businessThinking, it's possible
they don't believe the impact is that big.

- If we can wait that long, why not wait even longer? Maybe we
should do nothing.

- A lot will change between now and then. The problem may get
worse, or the opportunity may be lost. What makes that okay?

If exploring these concerns winds up giving you a red light, at
least you'll hit it earlier rather than later. A red light is not failure,
but making a red light needlessly and painfully more expensive is.
At least you'll have saved yourself from putting time and energy
into something that was going to be derailed anyway. You'll also
have saved the company money and time.

Enough of the Right People

The next step is talking about people. Everyone needs a sense of
how much effort will have to be put toward the project. Your discussion should include only rough numbers on *how many* people
and *how long* they will be involved. Make sure you get agreement
to have the right people in the right places (e.g., executive and
management support and a champion, so they can help you take
down the barriers as the project moves forward. You don't need to
get agreement about who those people will be, specifically; it may
be enough to say, "We will need someone with the competencies
(clout, experience, abilities) that Sarah has." You will also want to
talk briefly about relative allocation of time and people from internal versus external sources.

Don't cheat the solution by allowing anyone to pretend that the results will somehow magically appear without allocating the right amount of people's time and getting the right people to create or select the solution and successfully implement it. Any roadblocks to involving the right people will tend to be at the extremes— people will want either too little involvement or too much involvement.

If someone thinks that their people are too busy and can't be involved, and you think it is critical they be involved, you will have to talk it out. You might say something like this:

businessThink: I think we may have a problem. I am completely convinced that we can achieve the results we need, but there's no way we can do it if your people are not involved. If they're not involved there will be no buy-in, no knowledge transfer, and that could ultimately put the project results at risk. What do you think we should do?

On the other end of the spectrum, sometimes they want their people to do all the work. If you believe this is a problem, say so:

businessThink: I have a concern. It's been my experience that as a company we lack the technical expertise to do this work on our own. When there aren't enough people, or they're not the right people—regardless of whether they're someone else's people or your people—someone will be unhappy with the outcome. What do you think we should do?

One way or another, address the issues early and head-on. This isn't the time to let your ego stick out. Use your XQ to be courteous in the way you say things and be direct about the issues. Keep your focus on the mutual benefit you each want from the results, and separate people from the issues.

Show Me the Money

Up to this point, you've checked out time and people. Now you come to everyone's favorite part: *money*. If people have been nice and cooperative up to now, brace yourself, because it's about to get funky and weird. When it comes time to talk about m-o-n-e-y, the energy level cranks up a few notches, and people become unusually uncomfortable. It's a hard topic to bring up, and if someone else brings it up, it's a hard topic to talk about.

One major reason that it gets uncomfortable is because up to this point, it's all been talk—it's all been thinking. There may have been pressure to get it right, but now you're talking about actually *doing* something. People start to feel the pressure of the accountability for the investment. When it's only talk, people can walk away. When it's cash on the line, if it doesn't work, somebody's going to hear about it.

Think about the last major purchase you made, whether it was a car, a home, or a boat—whatever. When you were only thinking about what you wanted and were doing the legwork, how much pressure did you feel? Probably not very much. However, when they slid the papers in front of you to sign up for the payments, the pressure you felt inside probably changed just a little—or maybe a *lot*.

Another reason for this discomfort and dysfunctionality is the mistake of not differentiating between value justification and price negotiation.

Value justification is the process of getting agreement with people about how much they are willing and able to spend to get the results they want. It gives you answers to two questions: "*Can* they afford this?" and, "*Will* they afford this?"

Price negotiation is the process of making sure you're getting the best deal. Even though we are only going to talk about value justification, here is a quick example of both concepts so you understand the distinction between the two.

Let's say you're considering buying a new car. One of the first decisions you make is how much you want to spend. Let's say you decide you can spend $30,000; that's your *value justification*. No negotiation with anyone was required (except maybe between you and you). When you actually go into the marketplace, your price range may shift a little, but fundamentally, you have a range of how much you are both willing and able to spend. Establishing a range helps you narrow the selection of cars (solutions) you will consider. There's probably no need to be looking at a Mercedes on a $30,000 budget.

After a few test-drives, suppose you find the car you really want, and it costs $29,000. Now what do you do? You negotiate the price! The issue is not whether you can afford to spend $30,000 (or less)— you've already established that. The remaining question is whether you are going to spend $30,000. *No!* $29,000? No. You will keep negotiating until you feel you are getting the best deal. This is *price negotiation,* and it has nothing to do with what you can afford.

When you talk with others in your company, make sure that it is clear that you are only trying to establish how much people are willing to spend to get the results. In your effort to make the distinction with others, don't expect all the weird stuff to go away. Reactions to asking for money tend to divide people into two camps:

- Nickel-and-dimers.   If you can pry their fists open, even on big-time opportunities, they don't like to invest because they have a belief that everything should be free or cheap.
- Sugar daddies.   They have lived with the problem for so long, and the problem has been so painful, that they overreact and write a blank check—sometimes with very little discretion.

Nickel-and-dimers want the results—as long as it doesn't come out of their budgets, or as long as they don't have to give up any of their best people. Upon your request for cash, they may disavow any knowledge of you. They close their eyes tight and hope (which is their preferred method of choice) it will somehow fix itself or go away. It won't!

> Money is the walk of the talk. When you ask people to write the check or invest money, you will learn very quickly how serious they are—or aren't. People vote with their wallets. When you ask them to invest money, the message as to whether they believe in the solution is clear if they cough up the dough.

Who's Your (Sugar) Daddy?

On the other end of the spectrum, overspending occurs simply because everyone has experienced the excruciating pain of the problems for such a long time, or because they're salivating over the opportunity. They see it as a life or death situation, and they want the solution at any price. You'd think that a sugar daddy was funding the project when you see the vaults of money spent on things that don't return much value.

There is a significant problem with both the nickel-and-dime and sugar-daddy approaches. If you nickel and dime projects, you don't get the time and talent needed, and that directly affects the quality of the solution you're crafting. In spite of the fact that everyone puts in their best part-time effort, the results aren't achieved fast enough, if at all. It's not long before someone pulls the plug, and even the people who have done their best trying to scrape something decent together on a low budget get the blame. If the business case is strong, and you really do have a *should* in front of you, follow the age old adage: If it's worth doing, do it right, or don't do it at all.

On the sugar-daddy project, people start paying attention to the huge amounts of money being spent, and they begin to get panicky. The longer the project goes on, the more anxiety they feel about the results that are showing up. The expectations become so gigantic that nobody can deliver on the dream. Suddenly, they decide that the burn rate is too high for the results that are showing up, and someone pulls the plug before the project is completed.

Even though these approaches are at opposite ends of the spectrum, they end up in the same place—the project gets cancelled midstream for lack of results. In either case, the business loses.

Neither one of these approaches is very helpful. Slow down. Talk about the project and the needed investment as businesspeople. Now is definitely not the time to take off your business-Think hat. Use your XQ. Line up the business case and the thinking that went into it with the investment. Don't wait to test your assumptions about the investment required until you present your final proposed solution—unless, of course, you're wearing a bulletproof vest.

If the first time you try out an investment amount with the jury of decision makers is when they hear your presentation or read your proposal, you are *guessing,* and you will have wasted your own time and everyone else's. Find out early if your ideas about the size of the investment overlap, or if your colleagues are going to fall out of their chairs when you put a number on the table. When you give your final presentation, you can give the detailed, scrubbed-down numbers.

How Did You Come Up with That Number?

When you test a range of numbers with others, there are some predictable answers they will give you:

- A budget has already been established, and it's too small.
- They don't agree with your range. For whatever reason, their expected investment is less than yours.

Any time they come up with a number that's smaller than your number—if you can overcome the panic and keep your ego from rushing in to save you, gather your composure and calmly ask this question:

businessThink: Out of curiosity, how did you come up with that number?

This is an important question. Let this question roll off your tongue as if it is the most natural thing to be asking. You will be absolutely amazed at how little thinking and justification often goes into the numbers other people come up with, especially compared against the business case you have. Their responses to this question will usually fall into one of two buckets: *logistics* or *value.*

The Logistics Bucket

You don't want to be fighting a value battle if the reason is simply logistics, and vice versa. You can easily tell if their rationale is logistical by listening to the words they use. They're not saying it's not worth it; they're just saying they have some logistical constraints. For example, let's say you are trying to fund a companywide client relationship management (CRM) system for the sales force, and you take your case to the jury. When you make a request for the money, let's say $1.2 million, they respond with something like this:

Colleague: We don't have it. We only have $750,000 left in this year's budget.
businessThink: Okay, that shouldn't be a problem. How much do we have available in next year's budget?

Or, they may say this:

Colleague: That would be way past the share of what my division is authorized to spend.
businessThink: That's understandable. Other functions are going to benefit from the results of this project. It only seems reasonable to ask them to put up some money for the benefits they'll get.

Or this:

Colleague: We only have $600,000 to get started.

businessThink: Great. Let's say we get started and are success-ful—where would the rest of the money come from?

If you are really feeling quick and daring, you could also say, "Great. How much do you have available to finish?"

Once again, they are not arguing about the *value* of doing it, they just need to manage the logistics. If the reasons for resistance truly are logistical, they can easily be resolved with some creativity. Work on it together and solve it.

The Value Bucket

Sometimes reasons that sound logistical are really smoke screens for problems of perceived value. You have a roadblock, so you should deal with it now, before it deals with you later. For example, let's say you are trying to overhaul the order-entry system in your company to reduce the number of errors in product delivery to customers. After you present your case and ask for the money, someone says this:

Colleague: I think the impact on the company you're showing is overstated.

businessThink: Well, if I didn't have confidence in the impact, I'd question the investment myself. Let's revisit the numbers I came up with and see where we're off.

If they have some reason to doubt that the proposed solution will give them the results you say it can deliver, you might say this:

businessThink: I'm glad you're willing to say so. If I had doubts, I'd probably question any investment as well. Let's talk about your concerns.

If they have reason to believe there are other priorities that are higher than the one you're proposing, they would be fiscally irre-sponsible if they didn't say so. You're on the same corporate team. If you're both truly interested in the same thing (and you should be!), there's only one question you might have: Do the other pri-orities have a business case to compare against?

Colleague: I think we can get a better return by investing in the e-commerce project that's being proposed. It's a higher priority.

businessThink: If we can, we should. If we can get better return and results for the same money, we would be fiscally irresponsible not to do it. I completely respect that. I guess the only way we could get burned is if the other higher priorities don't have a business case that warrants the investment. At least we'll make a well-informed decision. Does that sound reasonable?

Taking a closer look at the investment, for any proposal, should serve to weed out the *coulds* and focus on the *shoulds,* even if the *coulds* are already in progress. It's bad business, and it's low-XQ, to take fiscal realities out of any analysis. If the return on any project is far less than another project can offer, you haven't helped anyone—you should kill the *could.* You can't make any solution happen with insufficient resources. Without paying attention, you can starve a strong solution, or dramatically dilute the return by overspending. *Think it through!* By talking straight and up front about time, people, and money, you will be able to get a solution that exactly meets the company's needs.

Once you have a ballpark estimate of what it will take to make the solution happen, you need to get everyone to make a decision, and that can seem deceptively simple. It's not, as the next chapter shows.

The businessThink Mirror

In the following test, read each statement and check the box that best describes you. Even though the statements are focused specifically on you, ask the same questions of your department, division, management or executive team, and company.

The businessThink Paying Attention Test

	Yes	On occasion	Pay attention
1. I encourage people to discuss a reasonable budget for a solution before the final solution is proposed or adopted.	❏	❏	❏
2. I diplomatically challenge people's beliefs regarding resources (time, people, money, etc.) that don't appear realistic.	❏	❏	❏
3. Before I craft a solution, I get agreement on the value justification for the solution.	❏	❏	❏

CHAPTER SEVENTEEN

Maybe-Proof Your Company

With strong businessThinking and the right amount of time, people, and money in place, maybe-proofing your company is the last thing you need to do to bring it home. The challenge is, when you consider how most companies make decisions, it's scary. What *does* it take to get a decision made in your company? Wouldn't you like to know? In an attempt to get a decision made, how often have you wanted to cry out, "Would someone—anyone—puh-leeease make a decision!"

In a recent study, over 40 percent of both professionals and managers cited the need for multiple approvals as the most common barrier to making a decision. Other common roadblocks included politics, changing priorities, and getting people to agree up front on what they want to accomplish.[1]

Nowhere do you see so many dysfunctional practices in one place as in decision making throughout an organization. Ego, hidden agendas, unnecessary delays, unwarranted confidence, edicts, urgency, functional blindness, positional or political power, fear, and poor preparation on the part of both the people needing the decision and those making it—and that's just to name a few.

To make matters worse, the process is inconsistent. It's not unusual to see a new process invented for nearly every decision. There are some good reasons for a unique process, but it's seldom a conscious decision. More often than not, the decision-making process *gets in the way* of helping anyone, including the company. There are a lot of things that go on inside a company and people that interfere with making good decisions. It's likely we won't be able to help with multiple approvals, but we can help with some of the other common roadblocks. And speaking of roadblocks . . .

Decision Hoops

A good friend of ours was in a meeting making a final presentation to a group of senior executives. He had done his homework and had prepared a very convincing presentation. At the end of his presentation, one of the executive vice presidents asked for more information. "Could you go back and rework these financials? I'd like to see an improvement of 2 or 3 percent in net profit during Years 4 and 5. Maybe you're underestimating the sales figures or you can figure out a way to get some economies of scale in the costs somewhere. Then we can get together in a few weeks and take another look at it."

Huh? He couldn't believe it. Changing numbers was going to really change the decision? Who couldn't pull up an Excel spreadsheet, replace the cell formulas, and come back with different numbers? Does it make sense to delay a decision for a few weeks and try to get everyone together again just to see a small change in the net profit figures? If 2 or 3 percent would make that significant a difference between whether you should do this or not, that's probably the decision anyway! He wanted to pull out his laptop right there, modify the numbers, and then ask for the decision. Rather, he relied on his XQ.

Our friend asked a very good question to move beyond a *maybe* syndrome that would simply delay making the decision. "I am happy to go do that, and I'm confident we can get creative and come up with some different models. Out of curiosity, let's imagine that I went back to my office, ran the new figures, and you were looking at those figures right now. Imagine that the figures are what you are asking for—an improvement of 2 or 3 percent in Years 4 and 5. Then what happens?"

"Well . . . then we would have to take a closer look at the market data you have. We would have to know more about how this stacks up against competitive offerings. We would have to talk it through as an executive team and see how everyone felt."

Our friend had already presented all that data. He was running into yellow lights and executive static.

> *Often, it feels as if decision makers are holding up hoops for everyone to jump through. The hoops may be visible or invisible, but it is important and possible to discover what they are.*

When the ones in need of a decision prove they have jumped through all the hoops, the decision makers hold up new hoops, with a whistle that says, "That was pretty good. I didn't think you'd make it. How about this hoop? Oh, and we forgot to talk about this hoop." Once in a while they light the hoops on fire, just for entertainment.

As our friend relayed this story to me (Dave), I couldn't help being reminded of an experience I had when I was about 13 years old, working at my dad's small printing shop. My dad loathed salespeople, especially bad ones. One day, while cleaning the office, I saw an aerosol spray can on the counter that looked pretty normal as cans go. When I picked it up, I was surprised to see a picture of a bull on the can, and underneath the picture in blue letters, the words "Bullshit Repellent." When I asked my dad about it, he told me that one of the salespeople walking into the office had handed it to him with the invitation, "If you feel the need to use this at any point during our conversation, feel free to do so." Dad had left it on the counter in plain sight for all the other sales types to see.

I wish I would have had a can for our friend. The guy needed it. So do a lot of companies.

> **The objective of a decision-making process is to make a good decision that is in the best interest of the company—*period*. There should be no other reason.**

The objective of the process of making a decision is not to make anyone look good, smart, superior or experienced. It's not to vindictively shut down people (or departments) you don't like or can't get along with. Nor is it to derail someone else's proposal so yours has a better chance of being adopted. Too often it feels like "decision murder" by committee, only in this case everyone *wants* their fingerprints on the gun. If the idea fails, everyone can point to someone else, and if it succeeds, everyone can claim victory. Again, the objective is to *make a good decision* that is in the best interest of the company. Everyone is on the same *company* team. This is not about personal (or departmental) agendas—it's about the business's agenda.

Make a Decision!

The biggest favor you can do for your company is to make sure everyone is committed to making a decision— not necessarily a yes decision, but a decision.

It shouldn't matter whether the decision is yes or no as long as it is truly in the best interest of the company. You need to find out from others what information they need that would allow them to feel comfortable deciding.

To get good information about what it takes to get a *yes*, be equally committed to the fact that *no* is an okay answer. Sometimes you're almost as addicted to winning or being told yes as you are to ego, solutions, and speed.

Making it okay for no to be an acceptable answer removes pressure and barriers and demonstrates a focus on objectivity. The key is to be invested in truth and not just getting a *yes,* or winning at all costs, which can sometimes put the well-being of the company at risk.

When people really feel no is an acceptable answer, they'll be more prone to be straightforward and give you good information. As soon as they feel you're trying to lead them to your solution, to get them to agree and pin them down, the ego alarm will go off, and you'll get less-complete, less-accurate information.

You can't get results if you, or your company, can't seem to make a decision. How often do decisions in your company get sucked into the maybe syndrome?

It's common to hear, "We just need a little more information, and then maybe we could . . . ," or "Could you narrow this proposal down just a little, and then we'll . . . ," or "I really need to run this by just a few more people before we move forward." We know you could add to the list—ideas are endlessly bantered, considered and talked about, checked in and out of committees, left on people's desks, and floated around for a while, but nobody ever makes a decision, and then the opportunity dies.

The ones presenting their business case aren't the only ones who need a decision—the company does! Don't waste people's time with endless requests for scenario optimization, more data, and more meetings when it won't have a material effect on the decision. Maybe-proof your company. Some organizations are simply incapable of making a decision. It's not necessarily because the solution itself is bad, but because *nobody* will decide (or else *everybody* has to decide). The process seems like an endless maybe. There are some big downsides to the maybe syndrome:

- By the time you've made a decision, the context of the situation has changed, and you have to start over again.
- You spend a ton of time and money considering and deliberating, and nobody ever decides.
- Decision cycles are too long.
- It's a huge challenge to clearly and concisely allocate resources.
- People get frustrated and give up on great ideas.
- Productivity comes to a halt as people sit around waiting on decisions.
- Other good ideas that are waiting in line starve to death.
- People become cynical that the company can't recognize or even move on a good idea when it's staring them down.
- You move too slowly as an organization and lose nimbleness and agility, ultimately resulting in lost competitive advantage.

What if you could cut through all the red tape? Imagine how effective people could be if they knew that after all the information was presented, people would be committed to making a decision. Imagine how differently both sides would approach the process if both sides knew they had only one shot at a decision. Knowing that many decisions don't get made because they are prematurely presented to the decision makers, who really *do* need more information, you would make sure you provided all the information they needed. Knowing that they wouldn't get another look at it, the decision makers would make it more clear what information they needed to see in order to make a decision.

To convert the downsides of the maybe syndrome into upsides, here is what you need to know:

- What are all the steps the organization will have to take so that the decision makers would feel comfortable and able to make a decision?
- What will they do or decide at each step in the process?
- What is the timing of each of the steps in the decision process?
- Who is involved in each step in the process, and what is their decision-making role?
- What information does each person need to see or hear that would allow them to feel comfortable in making a decision?
- What criteria will each person apply in making a decision?

The Holy Grid for Making Decisions

People thrash around trying to get answers to the preceding questions. For some reason, many people shuck and jive when it comes to getting and giving answers to these questions. To bring some order to the chaos, we've developed a template for the decision-making process. Regardless of where you are in the corporate food chain, this can bring some decision discipline. What holy water is to the ungodly, the "holy grid" is to the demons of maybe. *Demons begone!* Gathering this information in a specific sequence increases the likelihood of getting the information, as well as the ease of getting it and the accuracy of the information you get. It also increases the odds of getting a decision made. The maybe-proofing template is shown on the following page.

Here's how you work the holy grid.

THE HOLY GRID

STEPS	DECISION	WHEN	WHO	HOW

Get All the Steps

The burning question everyone wants to know about a decision process is "*Who* is really going to make the decision?" Not surprisingly, this is usually the first question people ask, and it's the wrong place to start. Starting out with any *who* question creates two problems:

- No matter how gently or innocently you ask the question, "So who's going to make this decision anyway?", it doesn't turn out the way you hope. The subtext is the only part of the question the other person hears, and it sounds like this: "Clearly it's not you. You are incapable of making this decision since you're [too low in the organization, too inexperienced, too young, too old, too dumb]. I want to talk to the *real* decision maker—someone important." Don't expect cooperation or good information if that's the question *they* think you're asking.

- The second problem you run into when you ask someone "So who's going to make this decision anyway?" is that they most often say, "I am." Few people are really *the* decision maker, no matter how they see themselves. Here's a case in point:

    There was a company that sold large, very expensive heating and air-conditioning systems for big office buildings, malls, and

THE HOLY GRID

STEPS	DECISION	WHEN	WHO	HOW

hotels. Some of these systems cost hundreds of thousands to millions of dollars. In an effort to help their salespeople shorten the sales cycle by getting to the decision makers faster, they hired an independent company to help them identify whom they should be targeting their selling efforts toward. They sent out a questionnaire to their clients—plant managers, maintenance supervisors, executive vice presidents, CFOs, and CEOs. One of the questions asked was "Who is really, ultimately responsible for making the purchase decision?" Each person responded, "I am." Most everyone is *a* decision maker. So even if it's true, it's often not the complete answer.

Removing the Emotional Land Mines

By asking about the steps *first,* you take some of the emotional reaction out of the situation, and help make getting the steps a straightforward process. Simply ask, "What are all the steps you (or we) will have to take to make a decision that is in the best interest of the company?" Note that you are *not* asking "What has to happen for you to decide in favor of what I am proposing?" If the people you are talking with get the sense that you are trying to lead them where they don't want to go, they will close down. Keep everyone's focus on the best interest of the company. In the spirit of mutual interest, make a list together of *each* of the go/no-go steps. Test the list to make sure you have not overlooked a single step, or you will be surprised and disappointed when you hit a snag.

By the way, the people you considered while exploring the ripple effect may have some input. Make sure to keep your functional as well as your big-picture hat on. Once you've checked everything out, you should have a complete list of steps. If it changes as you go, keep it current. The grid isn't carved in stone. If people are unclear as to the steps, suggest some that would make logical sense. Work it out together.

The Decision

The second column in the grid is the Decision column. You might say, "I understand all the steps we will need to take. Just so that I am clear, what *decision* gets made in each step?" The difference between the step and the decision is most easily understood as follows: Imagine that you have all the steps captured, and within those steps there are two different committees that are identified in each step. However, one is simply giving opinions on your proposal, and the other is choosing which project to fund. If you were allowed to meet with only one committee, which one would you want to talk to? It's likely you would talk with the committee that makes the decision.

THE HOLY GRID

STEPS	DECISION	WHEN	WHO	HOW

THE HOLY GRID

STEPS	DECISION	WHEN	WHO	HOW

The *When*

The third column to fill out in the grid is the When column. Each go/no-go step should have at least a tentative date. This is the date by which you think the step will be completed. Create an up-front agreement that the dates you identify will serve as checkpoints to make sure the decision stays on track. That way, if a date is missed, you can bring it to someone's attention and take the necessary steps to get back on track. You can't hold people accountable, nor will they feel responsible for the decision, if they aren't committed to the same timeline. This is basic, and if you don't nail it down you will regret it.

If timelines are missing or fuzzy, offer some dates that make sense. Don't be surprised if timing changes. Keep the dialogue about the changes and modifications open and ongoing.

The *Who*

Because you have identified the steps, the decisions, and the *when,* it will seem that asking "Who is involved in each step?" is the next, most natural question you could ask. Make sure that you identify all the people in each step and that no one is missed. Identify each person's decision-making role or the reasons they're involved in this step. You will need to talk to those people *directly* and find out how they see things.

THE HOLY GRID

STEPS	DECISION	WHEN	WHO	HOW

Getting the *How* from the *Who*

Finding out the criteria that will be applied in making a decision is the most important part of the decision process.

> *The goal—dare we say mandate—is never to make a presentation or a proposal to people whose criteria for judging you are unknown to you. There's no way around it—to do so is major-league guessing. The businessThink mantra is no guessing! This is the business version of no blind dates.*

The best way to understand what is important to the key stakeholders is to talk to them. When you get to see these people—and sometimes it's very difficult to get to see them—get to know the issues from their perspective and their criteria for making the decision. In other words, businessThink with them.

You want to know the distinctions between where the stakeholders *could* choose to spend their money and where they think the company *should* spend its money.

It is very common that their decision criteria will be unconscious, missing, or not well thought out. They may say that they want "proof that the system is easy to use." What would convince

THE HOLY GRID

STEPS	DECISION	WHEN	WHO	HOW

them? Just because they say the words doesn't necessarily create an understanding of their definition of *easy to use*. You might think it's easy to use, and they won't. Find out what would convince *them*. Based on your experience, you may be able to suggest criteria that would be helpful. Again, don't be afraid to ask them or offer to fill in what's missing.

Warning: Personal Stake at Risk

> Even though you are all supposed to be on the same corporate team and have the same objective, when you present your business case, people may make decisions in their own best interest, not necessarily in the organization's best interest.

Although businessThink is designed to expose this dysfunction and drive it out, we recognize the reality that many companies are politically charged, and that won't change overnight. If you can understand how people personally stand to win or lose, you have a chance to create a bridge between what's in their best interests and what's in the company's best interest.

In something as complex as business, there are almost always conflicting rewards and goals. If you can find out how people are personally rewarded for performance, and can tie the solution to their individual or functional wins into the bigger picture of the companywide solution, then the possibility of having your solution help the company, as well as the individuals affected by it, goes up exponentially. You may even have the opportunity to provide additional value by resolving conflicting objectives and priorities.

We know this is basic stuff. You don't have to be an astronaut to work the holy grid. However, don't mistake its simplicity for being simplistic. Sad but true: If you don't live by the holy grid, you will be defenseless against bad thinking and processes that can send a lot of great businessThinking into the abyss.

Note. **If you can make a difference, please read the following:**

If you are in a position to make your company's decision-making process better, *do it!* We beg you! Maybe-proof your company by doing the following:

- Consciously think through all the steps required to make a good, well-informed decision. Don't leave any step out. Don't arbitrarily add steps, and don't hide any. Make the process clear to everyone else and stick to it.

- Make sure that everyone understands what they are supposed to do and what authority they have to make a decision in each step.

- Establish realistic timelines as a target for each step in the process. If the decision gets off track, get everyone involved committed to getting it back on track.

- Make sure that everyone who needs to be there to decide is in the room. If they can't be there, get someone who can, or delay the meeting. In order for you and others to commit to making a decision, you need to be assured that those making presentations will give you all the information needed to make a good decision that is in the best interest of the company. Before the meeting, make sure that those making presentations can deliver on that requirement. If not, delay the meeting. The output must be a decision; otherwise, it's just another meeting. (Ahhh!)

- Be clear on what criteria will be applied in making a decision. If you fail to do this collectively and do not clarify each criterion, each person will apply their own criteria, which may or may not be clearly defined or helpful. This will make it hard for those making presentations to hit the target, and hard for those making the decision to come to consensus.

> *Decision-making would be revolutionized if there were better preparation on both sides, and you must be prepared to do it. It is building into your company a healthy quid pro quo— others commit to giving you all the information you need, and you commit to making a decision. Go! Move! Be bold! Just make a decision. Either yes or no is okay. If no is truly the right answer, then say so and stick to it. Just don't say maybe!*

Out On a Limb

This will not be very popular, but we're going to say it anyway: Stop having so damn many people involved in decision making! Eliminate unnecessary people—they often just slow the process down and make it more complex. Get the number involved down to the smallest possible irreducible number. Be lean, efficient, and effective. Lose the decision weight in your company. The time it takes to arrive at a decision, and the chances of actually making a decision, go down inversely to the number of people involved if it's more than three.

The businessThink Mirror

In the following test, read each statement and check the box that best describes you. Even though the statements are focused specifically on you, ask the same questions of your department, division, management or executive team, and company.

The businessThink Maybe-Proof Test

	Yes	At times	B.S. repellent needed
1. I think through, and help others think through, every step we must take to make a well-informed decision in the company's best interest.	❏	❏	❏
2. I establish a realistic timetable for each decision step, including the final decision.	❏	❏	❏
3. Before preparing a solution or proposal for others to approve, I speak with each person who may influence the decision.	❏	❏	❏
4. I do not hesitate to ask people's views on alternative solutions available inside and outside our company.	❏	❏	❏
5. I work to ensure we make the *right* decision, and not just a decision for activity's or speed's sake.	❏	❏	❏
6. I work to make sure we have enough information that we can make a yes or no decision, with no decision or maybe being suboptimal choices.	❏	❏	❏
7. Before presenting potential solutions, I obtain agreement on the desired objectives from all key people.	❏	❏	❏

Now that you've looked in the businessThink mirror for the last time in this book, you're equipped with information about how sharp your businessThink skills are and where you could stand to get a little better. Make sure the new awareness you've gained doesn't slip out of sight; revisit chapters where you've discovered your biggest challenges. As we mentioned earlier, for further self-assessment tests to help you take the next step, visit our Web site at www.businessthink.biz.

• CHAPTER EIGHTEEN •

The Age of *Now*

In the future, people will still matter to businesses, but some people will matter more than others. When Accenture recently interviewed 500 executives around the world and asked "What workforce skills are in most demand and will be most needed over the next two to five years?" this is how they answered:[1]

Business skills	68 percent
Technical skills	42 percent
Flexibility and adaptability	33 percent
Self-motivation	18 percent
Leadership	6 percent
Functional	3 percent

So the question is, would you like to become a functional, self-motivated leader, or a flexible, adaptable businessperson with great technical skills? People who can independently think on their feet, work cross-functionally, learn new skills quickly, and work to make great business decisions that are customer focused (for both internal and external customers) will be indispensable to their companies and in high market demand. By the way, executives not only said they expect to need these skills shortly, they also expect these skills to be *very* difficult to come by (good demand news for you in the supply and demand of labor economics—if you live the rules).

The *Now*

There are lots of great books written predicting the future of business and where it's headed; they're helpful in widening your perspective. There are a lot of books that tell us where we've been, and we can definitely learn from those. The focus of businessThink is slightly (maybe dramatically) different—businessThink is about what to do *now*—the compressed now. We aren't futurists, nor are we historians. We are the "nowists." *Now* is where the future is created and changed. *Now* is where you are—the present. Our not so subtle point is, *change the now.* You don't lead a business into the past, and you also can't lead the business next week or next year. Lead the business *now.* Lead yourself *now.* Leading the *now* will demand a new kind of businessperson.

Not to sound too harsh, but in business you are somewhere on a scale between a pure cost or a return on investment. If you're only a cost, your cost is too high. If you deliver a return, how high is it?

> There are volumes written that say there will be no more room for the average performer in the future. Not true. There is always room for the average—lots of room, and plenty of company. The question you have to answer for yourself is, "What do you want for yourself and your company?"

The average is there for the taking; not much is required to get there. Since your output is driven by your activities, and your activities are driven by your decisions, and your decisions spring from the well of your thinking, the thought to ponder is this:

How deep is your thinking? Your company's thinking? Is it the depth of a well or of the average Dixie Cup?

You are going to be put to the test repeatedly, not only to make fact-based decisions but also to make some sense out of all of the conflicting and hard-to-detect signals that come through the fog and the noise. Great businessThinkers are the ones who can handle a bunch of ambiguity, sort through it, and make great decisions.

> businessThinking is an opportunity to work through ambiguity and fail intellectually before the costs of building a solution get too high.

A massive challenge in making the right decision has been the long lag time between cause (ideas, decisions, choices) and effect (the success or failure those decisions produce). The gap stays far enough apart that you don't know whether what you're doing is right.

Half of all decisions succeed, and the other half fail. The mystery is in knowing which half is which.

The unsolved mystery takes its toll. Bridging the gap is what businessThink is designed to do. Running your decisions and ideas through businessThink helps you compress time and look at the impact of your decision.

> The rules of businessThink working together construct a little "black box" that compresses the time between cause and effect. If you slip a solution into the box, the box will move off the solution; grind through the evidence, impact, ripple effect, and constraints; and then screen out the impurities of bad ideas. The output moves you closer to the pure, on-target solution.

Instead of waiting weeks, months, or years to see if something works, what if you could compress all the thinking and results into a day? What would you learn, and how would it change your perspective?

When I (Steve) started my company, each partner fronted about $700 to get our company up and running. Not much of an investment or a big risk. Had you asked me about my businessThinking at the time, I would have said that I had it straight. Soon the infusions of cash needed just to keep the business going became larger and were needed more frequently. During my four years with the company, I hardly took a salary. Over time, when you add up my direct and opportunity costs, the amount exceeded $300,000 (not to mention the taxing mental and emotional costs). Had you asked me before I began if I was willing to bet over a quarter-million dollars on my businessThinking, and that of my partners, my answer might have changed.

If you could drop a decision into the little businessThink black box to have it rigorously think through the problem or opportunity, and then calculate the cost of starting and sustaining a business or a project along with the ultimate financial gain or loss of the business based on that thinking, the output would cause many decisions to change. It's also unlikely that 2,294 entrepreneurs would still sign up to start a new business every day without using it. It's also possible that many, many more would succeed because of using it. businessThink runs ideas through the black box before running them through the big bad bank account, and it bridges the gap between cause and effect so your decisions of the *now* deliver a better *future*.

Living in businessThink Nirvana

Speaking of the little black box, sometimes people, not just decisions, get run through it. I (Dave) had one such experience in a place I didn't expect. A few years ago, I had a very important job interview. There can be a lot of pressure on both sides in an interview; it's almost a microcosm of business. *You* (the candidate) are under pressure to get it right because the impact of succeeding or failing is big—*very* big. Your performance in an interview can affect your income, livelihood, career path, personal growth, and even your self-image. Because it's a competitive, "may the best candidate win," process, you'd better be on top of your game and in the zone.

They (the employers) are under pressure to find the right person for the position. Their choice will say something about their own ability to recognize and attract talent. Other people in the company will be watching closely and anxiously to see who they will be working with. As a result, the employers come to the interview with the traditional expectation that you will arrive ready to demonstrate your brilliance, tell them all about yourself (and your resume), and prove why you are the best candidate for the position. Any sign of weakness and you're out. Talk about pressure—both of you better get it right—now and no matter what!

In my case, all the usual pressure was compounded by what they wanted to get out of this critical position. This company had determined that the senior vice president of sales was performing poorly, and they'd fired him. Whoever they hired for this position was expected to be the heir apparent to the CEO, who had already announced his retirement in two years. They wanted to groom a strong leader for a few years to ensure that there would be no disruption in the business, and to increase the board's confidence.

I was interviewing with the chairman of the board. If you were interviewing with the chairman of the board, what would *you* say about yourself? On the drive over to their office, the anticipation got to me—my palms started to sweat, my anxiety skyrocketed, and my ego meter started to redline. I pounded the steering wheel and hyped myself to a frenzy with some self-talk. I was ready to do the fire walk with Anthony Robbins!

Luckily, while waiting in the lobby I got myself together. I know this will sound sick, but I now have the businessThink rules in my DNA. I had never applied the businessThink rules in an interview before, but why not try? Then it struck me—the request for a vice president of sales sounded eerily like a solution. The only things I didn't know were what that solution would solve and what opportunities it would help them achieve. I didn't have any evidence or impact. So, I decided I needed to move off the solution and committed to trying to apply the businessThink rules. (When you're interviewing for a position, you might imagine it's a bit difficult to move off the solution—especially when *you are* the solution!) Based on the outcome, I will never be the same. Here is the dialogue of that interview:

Chairman: Thanks for coming in, Dave. I've looked over your resume and am impressed. Tell me a little bit more about yourself.

Dave: Okay, I'll tell you everything you want to know. So that I can make my comments relevant, before we dig in to the details about me, do you mind if I ask you a few questions?

Chairman: I don't mind at all.

Dave: The vice president of sales is a pretty important position in your company. The last person in this position was recently fired. If you expect me to be successful and solve some of the problems in sales [moving off the solution as subtly as I knew how], it would be helpful if I knew a little bit about them. Out of curiosity, without getting into unnecessary details, what were all the *issues* that had to be dealt with due to poor performance?

The chairman brought up three or four that seemed to make pretty good sense:

- There had been a lack of accountability with the sales staff.
- He was out of touch with sales opportunities.
- His selling ability was generally weak.

I asked if there were any others. After a brief pause, he added a few more.

- Turnover in salespeople
- Unhappy people and bad morale
- Sales not working well with production

Dave: Of these things, which one would you say was the most important?

Chairman: I would say the biggest issue was the fact that he was out of touch with the opportunities our salespeople are working on.

Now I wanted to find some *evidence* that would prove the vice president had been out of touch.

Dave: What were some of the things that you noticed or experienced that let you know he was out of touch with what was going on?

Chairman: For the last year I've been hearing reports of big sales opportunities, and none of them have come to fruition. When I asked him where we were with some of these opportunities, I never got anything that was clear. He always seemed to have plenty to say, but I never got the feeling he was on top of it.

Dave: That makes sense. What else was there too much of that let you know he was not on top of things?

I watched his eyes as he gave me more evidence. It seemed he was getting great value out of our discussion. He described what he'd heard from others in the sales division and what a few customers had said, and he included some observations from the

CEO. Most of the evidence he offered was *soft*. I wanted to dig for some *hard* evidence, too.

Dave: This is really helping me understand what *not* to do, and is clarifying some expectations. Out of curiosity, when the vice president of sales is not on top of sales opportunities, then what happens?

Chairman: Salespeople that need help don't think that it's available. Some of them are somewhat new to our company, and they don't know all the ins and outs of what we can do. They need help to advance the sale. That causes us to lose momentum with the opportunity. It's too easy in our business for customers to go from being enthusiastic to uninterested.

He told me several other things that had happened as a result of the vice president not being on top of things. There was more soft evidence. I still needed to keep digging to see if there was any hard evidence.

Dave: So when you lose momentum and customers become uninterested, what do those things lead to?

Chairman: We're losing too many opportunities and not acquiring new customers. It's also causing some turnover with our salespeople, because they don't feel they can get the support they need.

We identified the impact of sales and turnover of salespeople (both being hard evidence)—to the tune of about $4 million or $5 million. That was the size of the problem the company was trying to solve. Now that we both knew the evidence, and the impact on the pain side, I wanted to explore the gain side.

Dave: This has been very helpful. I appreciate your sharing so much detail. Let's shift gears a bit. Let's say that you are able to find the perfect person for this position. Just so I don't miss anything, what are all the results you personally will expect him or her to deliver?

Again, he made a list. I had to prompt him to add anything else that might be missing, and he added a few items.

Dave: Of all of those things, if this person could only deliver on one of them, which one would you say is absolutely the most imperative?

He picked one of the issues, and my questions explored the evidence in depth.

Dave: One year down the road, what specifically will you be looking for as criteria that will let you know that this person really delivered what you need?

He paused, thought about it for a minute, and then shared his criteria. I still wanted more evidence, so I kept asking questions.

Dave: That seems as if it would be a good indicator. What *else* will you be looking at to judge whether this person was successful?

Once I had sufficient evidence, I started to search for the soft evidence to get to the hard evidence.

Dave: This is really making good sense to me. If you get all of those things in your business, help me understand what that will allow you to do as a business that you can't do today.

He described several things, some of which were hard evidence. Together we converted the nonfinancial data into money. We identified a $9- to $10-million impact in revenue. The last step was to slow down for yellow lights.

Dave: Out of curiosity, what has stopped you from addressing some of these issues before now?

Chairman: Hmmm. That's an interesting question. (*Pause*) I think we have been reluctant to give all the authority needed to salespeople because we have been burned in the past. We've given the authority to approve some of these deals to the VP of sales, but he has been too uninvolved. Also, the president has been focused quite a bit on the operational side of the business, and needs to step up the accountability on the VP.

In a flash 45 minutes passed by, and the chairman glanced at his watch and smiled.

Chairman: This has been an interesting interview on *our* company. When do I get to interview *you*?

Dave: You can ask me any question you want. Now I can tell you *more* about the parts of my experience that are most relevant to what you need as a business now, and what you are trying to accomplish long-term.

We talked for another half an hour and I left.

Experience on your resume is like the chapters in a book. I knew after the interview of the company which chapters he needed to read, and which ones would be a waste of time. Do you think the chairman would have allowed me to ask questions for 45 minutes if they'd been a waste of his time? He had to *think* before he could answer most of my questions. He had not thought in-depth about the story behind the pain or the gain. In less than an hour, I was able to develop a better understanding of what had happened in the past and what they hoped to have happen in the future. The impact of the pain and the payoff of the gain added together was roughly a $14- to $15-million proposition. If some-one had the skills to deliver those results, what would you need to pay? $80,000—or maybe $90,000—a *month?* As an outsider—an interviewee, no less—I added value to the chairman's business by the questions I asked.

In the end they offered me the position, and I kindly turned them down. That only made them crazy, and they kept coming back. They desperately needed someone who could cut through the issues, get to the most important one, and make sense of all the available information. A year and a half later, they were out of business.

In your pursuit of becoming the businessperson of the *now,* the better you get at living the rules, the better your results will be, personally and professionally. The results can even occasionally come at times and in places where you least expect them (like a job inter-view). However, that doesn't mean that if you aren't living all of the rules all of the time, you won't get some amazing results.

The businessThinking Hall of Fame

Imagine the impact of living just one rule: Check Your Ego at the Door. If you and those around you had no ego, imagine the impact that one rule would have on collaboration and communication in your company. We'll share some examples of people who have lived at least one of the rules to the point of near genius. It doesn't mean they're perfect, but it does show the power of applying just *one* rule. The examples shed some light on the power of *one person* living by the rules. We'll also share a couple of examples of when the rules all came together, and the specific results they delivered.

The businessThink Hall of Fame is for those who try, apply, experiment, dig deep, and persevere, not just those who live the rules to perfection (because nobody is perfect).

Inductee 1

Colman Mockler built the Gillette empire while modeling incredible humility and constantly checking his ego along the way. He used his humility as a powerful, unshakable tool in outlasting several hostile bids to take over Gillette. Some might believe that it was ego causing him to hang on to control of the company. Not so.

One of the takeover bids offered a 44 percent premium over the then-current stock price. It would have been easy for stockholders to flip their shares and pocket the quick gains. Mockler himself would have pocketed millions and could have retired in style. Most would have caved in to the temptation. Rather than surrender, Mockler made huge investments in the company's future in new technology and advanced innovations (the Sensor and Mach 3 razors), based on solid businessThinking. According to Jim Collins in *Good to Great* (a *great* book), if Mockler had let his ego get in the way and taken the easy benefit of the hostile buyouts, Gillette's stock would have been worth about $30 at the time of that writing (2001). In fact, that same stock was then worth $95.68.[2]

Mockler was a "quiet and reserved man, always courteous, [and had] a reputation of a gracious, almost patrician gentleman. Yet those who mistook Mockler's reserved nature for weakness found themselves beaten in the end."[3] Had his ego gotten in the way, it's unlikely Gillette would be where it is today.

Inductee 2

Jeff Hawkins has boundless curiosity, and it drove him to create one of the most successful products in history. In fact, maybe you're reading this book on his original invention: the PalmPilot. The PalmPilot is the fastest-selling consumer-electronics product in history. It broke the initial sales records of cell phones, pagers, and even color television sets. Where did that kind of success start?

Hawkins grew up in an environment where curiosity was encouraged and cultivated by his father. "My dad was always coming up with spectacular, impractical ideas," he says. "We were exposed to crazy things. But we learned to look at the world from all kinds of angles: mechanical, electrical, even business."[4]

If you *don't* cultivate and encourage a curious environment in your company and live the rules of businessThinking, you will lose people you can't afford to lose. In 1998, fed up with 3Com's limited vision for the wildly successful Palm, Jeff Hawkins and Donna Dubinsky resigned and within weeks founded Handspring.

Since their departure, Palm has yet to release a single device that hadn't been conceived by Hawkins. With Dubinsky as the businessThinking chief strategist and CEO, and Hawkins as the chief curiosity officer, Handspring introduced their first product, Visor, 14 months later and won a 21 percent market share in little more than a year. That helped knock Palm's market share down from 83 percent to 63 percent.[5]

Has all the success stifled Hawkins's curiosity? Not even close. "I want to solve the major problems in the study of human intelligence," he says. "I want to achieve a theoretical understanding of how the brain works. My research into human cognition is a life-long pursuit. It began before Palm, and it will last beyond Palm."[6] By the way, don't underestimate the chances that he'll do it.

Inductee 3

Living by the rules helped save one of the better-known brands in the world: MasterLock. If you don't know MasterLock, you would recognize the brand from a commercial that ran during the Super Bowl years ago, which showed a bullet hitting one of their locks, and not breaking it. The commercial conjured up an image of the unbreakable brand. Years later, the bullet still wasn't a problem—slipping market share was.

MasterLock's market share had dipped below 50 percent for the first time in years. The "bullet" was off-brand locks sold at a lower price (or so it appeared). Consumers were still buying padlocks, but they weren't connecting with MasterLock's products. The company needed something to revitalize the brand.

Enter the businessThinking company: Design Continuum. When Design Continuum started work, it would have been easy to just give MasterLock a "silver bullet"—some new designs, stronger branding, tell them to lower their price, and move on. In fact, this may have been what MasterLock wanted, asked for and expected. They didn't get that.

Design Continuum moved off MasterLock's requested solution to the underlying issues they were trying to solve with the lock itself—after all, a lock is a solution, but what problem was it solving? When the answer seems like a "duh" (like "locking stuff up") it takes a real commitment to move off the solution and ask a question that seems obvious. After moving off the 50-year solution, they got up and searched for evidence to see what showed up.

Design Continuum went out into the field, watched how real people use padlocks, and learned what consumers expect from a padlock. Intensely curious, they hung out at department stores and watched people buy locks. They watched people use locks. They studied "archetypes" of lock users and quickly discovered lifestyle-oriented segments: sporting goods, bicycling, home and yard, travel, school, gym, automotive.

While they were digging for evidence, they found that people don't care about the lock itself—people care about the stuff the lock was bought to protect. (Imagine that!) When you dig for evidence, you have to get out of your own head *and* out of the office (or your cubicle). If Design Continuum had just sat in an office and ruminated on possibilities through their functional expertise, they wouldn't have noticed the nuances.

Their research led to some nontraditional approaches in what they proposed to MasterLock. Based on the evidence and the impact to the consumer, they overhauled the lock's design and packaging. They changed the shape of the lock, eliminated the rough edges, moved the keyhole from the bottom to the front face (hallelujah!), and placed a rubber sheath around the lock to help prevent the lock from causing surface scratches on people's important, lock-worthy stuff.

They recommended that padlocks be placed in different sections of the store where people buy nonhardware goods, such as the home and garden or sporting goods sections. By making the locks more readily available and relevant to consumers' avid interests, they increased the perceived value of the MasterLock brand. They even changed the packaging to appeal to the hobbies of consumers and the valuables they want to lock up and moved away from images of the lock itself.

In essence, they injected life and functionality into something as cold, hard, and impenetrable as a steel lock. They also injected life back into MasterLock. By businessThinking, the net result has been the redesign and reinvention of an American icon, and MasterLock has been experiencing double-digit growth since.

Inductee 4

The rules work in real life, and you don't have to be Colman Mockler, Jeff Hawkins, or Design Continuum to make them work. A good friend of ours in Cornwall, England, shared with us how he, an average working stiff, can live the rules.

He worked for a small, cash-strapped start-up software company—the sort of organization where everyone's a vice president except the receptionist. (The receptionist was paid more money than anyone else because he alone refused to be compensated in stock options, but that's another story.) Anyway, their marketing maven said that all their customers were demanding that they rewrite their software from an OS/2 platform to Windows. Apparently, converting to Windows was nonnegotiable. It was going to happen, and the only questions were *when* and *how.* (Invoking "customer demands" is a common strategy, often aimed at putting the desired solution beyond challenge: "Personally, I'm entirely flexible; but the customer is always right, you know.")

Our friend was responsible for sales and administration—which included the coffee machine and the budgets—so he sat down with the programmers and the marketing people to try to figure out how much it would cost—in cash and in time—to develop a Windows version. In a case like this, he says, it was easy to check his ego: As soon as the geeks started talking, he understood about one word in three, and that word generally was either an expletive or the definite article. However, it didn't take long to discover that developing a new Windows version would take several months and about $50,000—which would mean most of the staff would have to be paid in stock options (again!) instead of cash. From this point, the conversation between the three of them went something like this:

Our Friend: So when we get this conversion thing done, then what? How does it help us?

Head Geek: Well, it doesn't help us as developers. We're much happier and much more efficient in OS/2, and Windows crashes a lot as well.

Our Friend: Okay, but what about our customers? How does it help them?

Head Geek: Good question. *(Pause for programmer refreshment: a Diet Coke, a Marlboro Light, and three Snickers bars.)* I guess the big thing is that all the other software our customers use is in

Windows, so the feel of a Windows interface is what they expect.

Our Friend: Anything else?

Head Geek: Well, some of them would like to be able to go in and change stuff around. But they're not allowed to do that anyway—it's part of the licensing agreement.

Our Friend: Anything else?

Head Geek: Not really.

Our Friend: Okay, so how big of a deal would it be for a customer to have this "feel of a Windows interface"? *(Our friend says it was easy to use the geek's exact words, as he had no idea what they meant.)*

Head Geek: For the novice users, it's quite a big deal. It would save them a lot of time.

Our Friend: And would that translate into more sales for us?

Marketing Maven: No question. A few at least. *(Pause)* Or maybe not; but it would stop our current customers from complaining.

Our Friend: Okay, and when our customers complain, then what happens?

Marketing Maven: Well, actually—actually it *is* only the new users who complain. So normally we spend about half an hour on the phone with them, give them a bit of coaching, and then they're okay.

Our Friend: Half an hour per new user. Roughly how many new users do we get—in a month, say?

Marketing Maven: Wow. Maybe one or two. So I guess, worst case, the current setup costs us about an hour per month. No big thing.

Our Friend: Right. And would there be any other implications?

Head Geek: Yes, if we did a Windows version, they'd complain about their systems crashing all the time. Give them OS/2 and they'll complain that it doesn't feel like Windows. Give them Windows and they'll complain that it doesn't perform like OS/2.

Marketing Maven: But we still have to go to Windows. We promised our dealers, and we promised our biggest customers. There's no way we can back down.

Our Friend: Wow, I'm a bit confused right now. What I'm hearing is that it really doesn't make sense to go to Windows, but that we have to do it to keep our promise. Help me out: Is there any way to have this whole thing make sense?

Head Geek: Sure there is. The dealers and customers don't care whether we run Windows, OS/2, or the Boston Marathon. All they care about is the interface, what the software feels like.

Our Friend: So here's a question for you as a software expert: Can you have the software written in OS/2 but make it feel like Windows?

End of story: The programmers developed what they called a *shell*. It took about a month to develop, and cost very little indeed—about $5,000. It gave the end-user a Windows interface, without changing any of the underlying OS/2 code. Novice users operated the software through the shell; power users went straight into OS/2. Because they did not change the underlying code, there were no problems with crashing.

No matter what company you work for, the size of the company, or what industry you live in every day; no matter if you are in a staff-level position or are a line manager, a senior executive, an up-and-coming CEO, or a first-time entrepreneur: The rules work.

Being an indispensable businessperson will no longer be determined solely by how much technical knowledge you have. Although that will still be a factor, you are now equipped for bigger and better things. In the era of knowledge work, which has long been predicted and has now arrived, your ability to *think* will be your competitive advantage. If you live businessThink, you will become indispensable in your organization. You will be one of the few bringing high XQ to the business. If you look around, you will notice a shortage of that type of talent. There will always be a place for those who are at the top of their game, who are "on" or "in the zone" most of the time. businessThink can put you in the zone by balancing your technical brilliance with solid business judgment. The trends of the past, present, and future all reveal the need for great businessThinking. If you have it, you will be in demand.

So how do you get wired for the *now* of businessThink? Is it just a gift? DNA? No—you just practice. When? *Now! Live it!* Make no excuses. Ease up on yourself when you make a mistake, and start again tomorrow. Live another day and try again. Nobody's perfect, but that's the goal. Peter Drucker once said that "All grand strategies eventually degenerate into work." Let the grand degeneration begin!

Good luck! Tell us how it goes for you. E-mail the authors at businessThink@hotmail.com.

• Q&A FOR THE BUSINESSTHINK CURIOUS •

In our presentations and consulting work, clients often ask us questions to deepen their understanding. In that spirit, here are some frequently asked questions that may deepen your perspective and enable you to better apply businessThink in your world.

Q. How does businessThinking fit with my technical expertise?

A. Picture your functional expertise as a software program on a computer. Each functional role in a company has its own icon on the desktop. businessThink is like the DOS or Windows operating-system software that runs the computer. businessThink is a mental operating system used *in conjunction with* your functional expertise software. If the operating system is slow or outdated, the functional software doesn't run as well, if at all. Or, if the operating system is fast, everything runs at maximum speed.

businessThink makes you do whatever you do better. It replaces your old method of thinking while helping you to collaborate with colleagues to leverage all of the functional brilliance and technical expertise your company has to offer. Use it to think through your branding and marketing strategy, human resources policies, operational structures, sales strategy, or management vision. Just add the word *Think* to all of these functions and change them for the better forever.

Q. What will be the reaction of others when I start to business-Think?

A. When you start applying businessThink in what you do every day, don't be surprised if others don't throw their arms wide open and embrace your new practice immediately. The first time you move off a solution and start to make a list of issues, it's likely they won't even notice. Or they will look at you and wonder, "What the hell . . . ?" Others are used to *you* finding answers a certain way; they have you all figured out. You will be upsetting their image of how you approach business by thinking, talking, and doing things differently. Even if only subconsciously, they will eventually recognize that you're changing; ultimately, if you change and they don't, it may create some discomfort. No one wants to be left behind. They'll sometimes resist.

Involving others in your new approach may help cut down on the resistance they'll feel. If they understand where you're coming from, it gives you a chance to show how you're trying to help them succeed. You can say, "I've been learning a few ways to raise the level of my thinking to help the business. Maybe it won't help, maybe it will. I'd at least like to try it, and we can make a decision together as to whether it's helpful." Let them in on your secrets and tell them exactly what you are doing; don't make it a mystery. businessThink is intended to be *inclusive,* not exclusive. They probably will see it as helpful when the results yield the right solutions every time, but *they* can always go back to doing what *they* have always done.

Q. **Does businessThink only work in certain situations?**

A. Don't be afraid to apply your new way of thinking to any scenario. There are very few instances in which you can't use the tools to your benefit, regardless of your role and the desired outcome. For example, we once used businessThink to get better clarity in defining end-user requirements on a new order-entry system. In this case, if someone says, "The system has to be easy to use," you can ask, "What evidence would you have to see that would prove to you that the system *was* easy to use?" Then your next question could be, "If the system was easy to use, what would that allow us to do as a business that we can't do today?" And you'll start to get access to information about impact.

Customer service people can use businessThink with customers who call in with complaints. It will help you understand the customer better by asking, "Just so I don't miss anything, what are all the issues you would like me to address today?" Make a list of all the issues, find out which one is most important, gather some evidence, and understand the impact. In this case, it's sufficient to understand the personal impact, and it would probably be best if you don't push customers to identify some economic impact.

You can even apply businessThink to areas of personal interest. For example, my wife and I (Dave) just built a large custom home. We designed the plans from scratch and took them to an architect and an engineer. Applying the rules of businessThink to the important elements of our home helped my wife and I analyze what was most important to us. We thought through the evidence that would let us know we got what we wanted, and we even identified the impact of getting those things. By applying business-Think rules to building our home we had a very successful experience: We built it in less than six months and went over budget by only 4 percent.

There is one area in which you must use businessThink with caution: You do have to be careful applying the rules in personal relationships. Make sure your intent is transparent, or you're dead! The intent of your questions, and your thinking, will matter—a lot. One day I (Steve) came home late from work and hadn't called ahead of time to let my wife know I would be late. When I came home, I realized my being late had put her behind schedule for an important meeting. She was trying to get out the door, and I made a cursory attempt at showing empathy (not my real intent) by attempting to give voice to her thinking. Getting to the real issues and bringing them into the open is right in line with business-Thinking. My real goal, however, was to avoid having to deal with the "discussion" later.

I said, "It looks like you're really mad that I'm late."

She said, "Don't give me that businessThink crap!"

Since that day, I highly recommend approaching the investigation of problems as they come up with the right intent.

The rules still work incredibly well when you're living them sincerely. We've used it in our marriages, in talking through issues with our children, in making large purchases, in solving community problems, and in closing big sales, and it works. When it hasn't, we've always been able to find where we didn't completely live one of our own rules.

Q. What are the traps you can fall into when you're business-Thinking?

A. You may be tempted to start processing people like information, as if they were inanimate objects. If you lose sight of the fact that people are feeling, thinking human beings, there will be the wrong intent. Your curiosity will be gone, and so will the soul of businessThink. No one will like it, and you will fail.

Another trap is mistaking features and benefits for real issues. Even we fall into that one occasionally. We had a colleague once who thought we needed a director of learning and reinforcement. His vision and goals for having that person were strong, and so we all started to list the important capabilities the person we hired would have to have. We quickly realized we had missed the point, which was to businessThink the issues first, and then develop the needed criteria for the person's qualifications. We needed to slow down and come up with a better-thought-out list that focused on the issues we needed to address rather than the competencies of the person we wanted to hire. Make sure you businessThink first, and then discuss the technical issues to deliver on the business issues.

Q. What did you do to get good at this?

A. I (Dave) once made a decision that I was going to get good at applying these rules. After I made that decision, the rest was pretty straightforward. I applied it to every conversation I had, whether I was meeting with customers or in a team meeting talking about some problems we were trying to address. Apply it. Use it. It simply works, and repetition is the only thing that will increase your ability to do it well.

Q. Isn't it possible that I could start to get a reputation as a naysayer or a person who just wants to think and not get it done?

A. The good news is that businessThink is so commonsensical that if you have your ego checked at the door, *everyone* will have a better chance of success if you live the rules. At some point, businessThinking will be instinctive and won't take too much time.

People will respect what you're trying to accomplish even if your technique still needs perfecting. Success doesn't mean that everyone will fall over in awe when you walk them through each and every step perfectly. They might not know, understand, or appreciate what you are trying to do. You didn't know any differently until you learned what to do, and that's *okay.*

Q. What if my businessThinking seems a little rough when I first start to try it out? Won't that cause me to lose credibility?

A. Don't get hung up on the fact that you aren't smooth at applying the rules. You won't be perfect, and that's not a reason not to do it. In the beginning, it's normal to feel a little out of sync and not in your usual flow. Repetition will make that go away quickly. It shouldn't take you too long to get this down to a science—usually three or four months if you consistently apply the rules. Besides, chances are your colleagues won't know how to business-Think, so they won't slap your hand and say, "How come you asked an impact question before you gathered all the evidence?" They won't know if you have taken something out of order.

Q. Do you have to follow the rules in a specific sequence?

A. It's true that there is some order to the businessThink rules, but in general, you can start anywhere you want. They don't have to be done in a linear sequential fashion in order to work. Some things wouldn't make sense if they were taken out of order, but it's not a fatal flaw if you do so. For instance, it doesn't make much sense to gather evidence unless you're doing it on the most important issue. Or, you can consider the ripple effect anytime you want; it just may make more sense if you do it after you completely understand all the issues, the evidence, and the impact.

Be prepared to be flexible when gathering information, because the people you're talking with will usually answer with whatever comes to mind. Let the dialogue flow naturally. It's completely normal that sometimes when you ask for evidence you'll get an impact answer. Sometimes you'll ask for impact and you'll get evidence. It's not so much the question you ask as the answer you receive that matters. Just capture the information and analyze it later, when you can refer back to this book if necessary.

Q. Does businessThink take a long time?

A. No! businessThink speeds things up when they need to be sped up. It slows things down when they should be slowed down. It creates the "about-right" speed. As a result, you will have fewer train wrecks to clean up, because your decisions will be better. Although the title of this work is *businessThink,* it represents a strong bias for action. The action of businessThink is what you do while you're doing—whatever it is you're doing. The challenge is in addressing *what you are going to do*—now, tomorrow, or next week. If your team gets businessThink into its culture, you will be able to communicate in businessThink shorthand.

Q. How do you handle it when others don't businessThink?

A. By businessThinking! Those around you don't have to change for you to enact businessThink. They don't need to know what you're doing or even that you're doing something—you just need them to answer the questions *with* you. When they answer them, you will all learn together. It may help you to realize that you're not wandering into the wilderness of the unknown and untested. This methodology works, and has been proven over and over again by thousands of people around the planet.

Just because it works doesn't mean people will play along. If the people in your company won't, you have two choices: Play or don't play. You can try to change the environment, and if it doesn't change, you have two other choices: Complain about it or get out and go to work for someone who gets it.

• NOTES •

Introduction

1. U.S. Patent Office, www.uspto.gov; Small Business Administration, www.sbaonline.sba.gov or www.getfacts.com.
2. Small Business Administration, www.sbaonline.sba.gov or www.getfacts.com.
3. Small Business Administration, www.sbaonline.sba.gov or www.getfacts.com; Dun and Bradstreet, www.dnb.com; U.S. Department of Labor, www.getfacts.com.
4. Robert McMath, *What Were They Thinking* (New York: Times Books, 1998), introduction.
5. Tom Peters, *The Circle of Innovation* (New York: Knopf, 1997), p. 76.
6. Peters, p. 76.

Chapter One

1. "Frederick Taylor, Early Century Management Consultant," *Wall Street Journal Bookshelf,* 13 June 1997, p. A17 (online); Frederick Winslow Taylor, "The Principles of Scientific Management," paper delivered to the American Society of Mechanical Engineers, 1911.
2. Alan Taggart, "Smart Companies, Dumb Decisions," *Fast Company,* October 1997, p. 160; Paul C. Nutt, *Making Tough Decisions* (New York: Jossey-Bass, 1989).
3. Kepner-Tregoe, *Decision Making in the Digital Age: Challenges and Responses* (Princeton, NJ: Kepner-Tregoe, January 2001).
4. Richard Foster and Sarah Kaplan, *Creative Destruction: Why Companies That Are Built to Last Underperform in the Market—and How to Successfully Transform Them* (New York: Currency Doubleday), pp. 7–8.
5. Mark Sirower, *The Synergy Trap* (New York: Free Press, 1997), p. 17.
6. Associated Press, "Dot.com Retailers in Trouble," New York, 13 April 2000, www.cnnfn.com.
7. Small Business Administration, www.sbaonline.sba.gov or www.getfacts.com.
8. Dun and Bradstreet, www.dnb.com.
9. Robert McMath, *What Were They Thinking?* (New York: Times Books, 1998).
10. Charles Bowden, *Blood Orchid* (New York: Random House, 1995).
11. Stewart Alsop, "The Tragedy of Webvan," *Fortune,* 13 August 2001, p. 52.

12. Tom Peters, *The Circle of Innovation* (New York: Knopf, 1997), p. 158.
13. Kepner-Tregoe.
14. Anna Muoio, "Unit of One," *Fast Company,* October 1998, p. 106.
15. Muoio, p. 107.

Chapter Two

1. Alan Taggart, "Smart Companies, Dumb Decisions," *Fast Company,* October 1997, p. 160; Paul C. Nutt, *Making Tough Decisions* (New York: Jossey-Bass, 1989).
2. Jack Welch and John Byrne, *Jack: Straight from the Gut* (New York: Warner Business Books, 2001), pp. 217–222.
3. Bill Breen, "Trickle Up Leadership," *Fast Company,* November 2001.
4. K. Patterson, J. Grenny, R. McMillan, and A. Switzler, *Better Than Duct Tape* (Plano, TX: Pritchett Runnler-Brach, 2000).
5. Jamie Oliver, "By Design," *Real Business Magazine,* October 2001, pp 33–39.
6. Joe Thomas, "Magnify, Filter, Alter, Fabricate," Power of Understanding Training, Franklin Covey Co.
7. Annette Simmons, *The Story Factor* (Cambridge, MA, Perseus, 2001), p. 51.

Chapter Three

1. Jim Collins, *Good to Great* (New York: HarperBusiness, 2001), p. 27.
2. Chester Karraas, *Give and Take* (New York: HarperBusiness, 1998), pp. 108–109.
3. FranklinCovey 7 Habits 360 Research, Franklin Covey Co., Salt Lake City, UT, 1989–2002.

Chapter Four

1. Grace Hopper, www.inventorsmuseum.com/GraceHopper.htm.
2. "The Deep Dive," *Nightline,* ABC News, July 1999.
3. Tom Kelley and Jonathan Littman, *The Art of Innovation* (New York: Currency Doubleday, 2001), p. 32.
4. Eric Hoffer, *The Ordeal of Change* (New York: Buccaneer Books, 1976).
5. Thomas Gilovich, *How We Know What Isn't So: The Fallibility of Human Reason in Everyday Life* (New York: Free Press, 1991), p. 82.
6. Jack Welch and John Byrne, *Jack: Straight from the Gut* (New York: Warner Business Books, 2001), pp. 182–183.
7. Peter Drucker, *The Effective Executive* (New York: HarperBusiness, 1966), p. 53.
8. Anita Roddick, *Business as Unusual* (London: Thorsons, 2000), pp. 37–38.

Chapter Five

1. Daniel Goleman, *Emotional Intelligence: Why It Can Matter More Than IQ* (New York: Bantam, 1995), pp. 81–83.
2. Goleman, p. 83.
3. Michael Warshaw, "Have You Been House-Trained?" *Fast Company,* October 1998, p. 46.
4. James C. Collins and Jerry I. Porras, *Built to Last* (New York: Harper-Business, 1994), p. 55.

Chapter Six

1. Thomas Davenport, *Information Ecology, Mastering the Information and Knowledge Environment* (New York: Oxford University Press, 1997).
2. William Issacs, *Dialogue, A Pioneering Approach to Communicating in Business and in Life* (New York: Doubleday, 1999), p. 43.

Chapter Eight

1. Marty Bates, Syed S.H. Rizvi, Prashant Tewari, and Dev Vardhan, "How Fast Is Too Fast?" *McKinsey Quarterly* no. 3, 2001.
2. Kepner-Tregoe, *Decision Making in the Digital Age: Challenges and Responses* (Princeton, NJ: Kepner-Tregoe, January 2001).
3. Polly Labarre, "Do You Have the Will to Lead?" *Fast Company,* March 2000, p. 222.
4. James Daly, "Interview with Alvin Toffler," *Business 2.0,* September 2001.
5. Bates, Rizvi, Tewari, and Vardhan.
6. Marcus Buckingham and Curt Coffman, *First Break All the Rules* (New York: Simon & Schuster, 1999), p. 133.

Chapter Nine

1. R. Pirsig, *Zen and the Art of Motorcycle Maintenance* (New York: William Morrow, 1974).
2. Thomas Gilovich, *How We Know What Isn't So: The Fallibility of Human Reason in Everyday Life* (New York: Free Press, 1991).

Chapter Ten

1. Henry Mintzberg, *The Rise and Fall of Strategic Planning* (New York: Free Press, 1994), p. 24.
2. Mintzberg, p. 77.
3. Tom Peters, *The Pursuit of WOW!* (New York: Vintage, 1994), p. 77.

Chapter Thirteen

1. Alan Taggart, "Smart Companies, Dumb Decisions," *Fast Company,* October 1997, p. 160; Paul C. Nutt, *Making Tough Decisions* (New York: Jossey-Bass, 1989).

Rule 8

1. Alan Webber, "Danger, Toxic Company," *Fast Company,* November 1998, p. 152.

Chapter Seventeen

1. Kepner-Tregoe, *Decision Making in the Digital Age: Challenges and Responses* (Princeton, NJ: Kepner-Tregoe, January 2001).

Chapter Eighteen

1. Accenture, *Key Skills for the Future, Human Performance Study,* 2001, www.accenture.com.
2. Jim Collins, *Good to Great* (New York: HarperCollins, 2001), pp. 22–25.
3. Collins.
4. Pat Dillon, "This is Jeff Hawkins on Brains," *Fast Company,* June 1998, p. 104.
5. Dillon.
6. Dillon.

• INDEX •

• ABOUT FRANKLINCOVEY •

FranklinCovey is a leading learning and performance services firm assisting professionals and organizations in measurably increasing their effectiveness in leadership, productivity, communication, and sales. Clients include 80 of the Fortune 100, more than three-quarters of the Fortune 500, and thousands of small and midsized businesses, as well as numerous government entities. Organizations and professionals access FranklinCovey services and products through consulting services, licensed client facilitators, one-on-one coaching, public workshops, catalogs, more than 173 retail stores, and www.franklincovey.com. More than 3,500 Franklin-Covey associates provide professional services and products at 44 offices in 38 countries.

The maniacal mission of businessThink is to help people build their capacity to independently think on their feet, work cross-functionally, learn new communication skills quickly, and work to create value by making great business decisions that get long-term *and* short-term results. businessThink learning transcends functions and teaches people to use the rules as the acid test for every product researched and developed, idea funded, alliance formed, merger contemplated, sales call initiated, operational overhaul implemented, management theory espoused, and strategy adopted. Learning to live the rules leads to better allocation of resources, strategic decision making, mapping products and services to targeted business results, solving critical problems, and choosing the right priorities.

For more information, call FranklinCovey at **(888) 972-6839;** for international calls, **001-801-817-7045;** or fax **001-801-342-6664;** or visit our Web sites, **www.businessthink.biz** and **www.franklincovey.com/businessThink.**